61

20,95
80u

ARTISTIC INTELLIGENCES

Implications for Education

*Published with the assistance of
the Getty Center for Education in the Arts,
a program of the J. Paul Getty Trust*

ARTISTIC INTELLIGENCES

Implications for Education

Edited by

WILLIAM J. MOODY

Teachers College Press
New York and London

Published by Teachers College Press, 1234 Amsterdam Avenue, New York, NY 10027

Grateful acknowledgment is offered to the following for permission to reprint the poems indicated:

"In the Waiting Room" from THE COMPLETE POEMS 1927–1979 by Elizabeth Bishop. Copyright © 1971 by Elizabeth Bishop. Copyright © 1979, 1983 by Alice Helen Methfessel. Reprinted by permission of Farrar, Strauss & Giroux, Inc.

"Six Significant Landscapes" from *Collected Poems* (1982) by Wallace Stevens. Reprinted by permission of Alfred A. Knopf, Inc.

"Torso of an Archaic Apollo" by Rainer Rilke from *Selected Poems,* trans./ed. by C. F. MacIntyre. Copyright © 1940 1968 C. F. MacIntyre. Reprinted by permission of the University of California Press.

Library of Congress Cataloging-in-Publication Data

Artistic intelligences : implications for education / edited by
    William J. Moody.
        p.   cm.
    Papers from the Artistic Intelligences Conference, held at the
University of South Carolina, Columbia, Apr. 20–22, 1989.
    Includes bibliographical references and index.
    ISBN 0–8077–3050–5 (cloth : acid-free paper)
    1. Arts—Study and teaching—United States—Congresses.
2. Students—United States—Intelligence levels—Congresses.
3. Creative thinking (Education)—Congresses.   I. Moody, William J.
II. Artistic Intelligences Conference (1989 : University of South Carolina)
NX303.A724   1990
700'.7'073—dc20   90-42042
                                                                                        CIP

ISBN 0-8077-3050-5

Printed on acid-free paper
Manufactured in the United States of America

97 96 95 94 93 92 91 90   8 7 6 5 4 3 2 1

Contents

Preface

The University of South Carolina's President James B. Holderman designated 1988–89 as "The Year of the Arts," during which the university honored artists and celebrated their creations. The academic focal point was an Artistic Intelligences Conference held in Columbia, April 20–22, 1989. Its purpose was to call the attention of educational leaders, and through them the general public, to the theory of multiple intelligences, developed by the noted Harvard psychologist Howard Gardner.

The implications of Gardner's theory were addressed with special attention to the role of the arts in education. Typically, our elementary and secondary schools concentrate on only two of the seven intelligences described by Gardner. Conference speakers urged delegates to implement strategies for improving general education in the United States so students can develop all their intelligences. Delegates looked for ways to convince educational leaders that students should be given opportunities to recognize strengths and, building upon them, the freedom to choose professions.

A musician might think of the conference as an introduction; Gardner's theory as the main theme; and this book, which includes the proceedings of the conference, as a segue to the development section that will be composed by educational leaders throughout the 50 states. The opus will be complete when our schools educate the several intelligences while helping students develop their special abilities.

Experienced teachers of the arts know that some students are "talented," making it easier for them to excel. During the conference, Howard Gardner was asked about his calling "talents" by another name. He responded that nomenclature was not something he would quibble about if natural ability in linguistics and in mathematics were also called talents. The roses that smell sweet in our culture are labeled "intelligence(s)," and Gardner's theory identifies at least seven, including those practiced by the "talented."

The contributors and I hope that this book will serve as a resource and catalyst for those who believe in educating the several intelligences and are willing to work for educational reform. Never before have the arts played such a prominent role in our culture. And never before have so many well-wishing leaders (political, business, and other) offered advice about our schools that actually endangers arts education. There are many problems in the schools, social and curricular, but the newsmakers usually advise simplistic solutions that only worsen the situation.

Throughout the years of the cold war, education was influenced by those who were concerned that Russia might "bury" us. Today, students are being returned to the basics so the United States can compete with Japanese technology lest we be buried by computer chips. Unfortunately, some influential, well-meaning but misguided leaders are returning students not to a liberal arts tradition but to a narrow focus on "what's good for business." Education must be more concerned with the quality of living than with the earning of it. And yet schools have always responded to societal forces, including political and business concerns; fortunately, the idealism of the populace is also an energizing force in this democracy, where all shall be equal under the law. The schools represent vision, hope, and faith that education will lead our children along the way to a better life. Education in the future will look quite different if we educate all the intelligences and maximize individual strengths as they are discovered. In *On Liberty* (1859), John Stuart Mill reminded us that "human nature is not a machine to be built after a model, and set to do exactly the work prescribed for it, but a tree, which requires to grow and develop itself on all sides, according to the tendency of the inward forces which make it a living thing."

When school administrators and teachers respond to educational critics and the public mania about standardized testing by preparing students for the questions on the test, scores do increase slightly. It is not reasonable to believe, however, that great things will happen when the mean score on the SAT increases from 750 to 790. Yet there is reason to believe that a bright future awaits students who develop their natural abilities and cultivate personal interests. Cultural literacy is a notable goal (among several) for education, with higher test scores a by-product. Although testing can tell us something about accomplishment in the academic areas tested, the data are often interpreted carelessly. The current overemphasis on test results produces anxiety in teachers and young people, and leads to a joyless school environment. Excessive concern for test results places the curriculum in a straitjacket and allows little energy or courage to pursue educational reform that recognizes several intelligences, different learning styles, and individual potential.

Professional teachers today have the opportunity to know more about the learning process than ever before. They can study books written by master teachers and benefit from educational research. But school systems are conservative, and changes come slowly (in part, because both teachers and parents remember their own schooling with nostalgia). Teachers find it difficult to make changes suggested by the professional literature, when they are faced with societal pressure to introduce material too early in the learning sequence and to force feed educational spinach in place of a balanced diet. They may know about learning styles but they do not have the time or skills to approach classroom instruction from many directions. The level of interest and support for education by the general public is encouraging; professional teachers need to show the way to use this energy productively. The speakers at the Artistic Intelligences Conference presented convincing arguments that the arts teach us in special ways and lead to understanding on many levels. Gardner's theory points out the need for new directions in what we teach and how we go about it.

The delegates to the Artistic Intelligences Conference were inspired by the speakers and collegial discussion at the three-day event. For instance, one participant told me that, in her 14 years of attending conferences, this was the most stimulating. I was also exhilarated at the time, and even more so while working on this book, which includes the speeches presented to the delegates; the ideas generated by the speakers seem even more powerful when read and pondered.

From my perspective as a musician, I conceived of the organization of this book in a modified sonata-allegro form, with "artistic intelligences" as a leitmotiv. Part I presents thematic material, Part II is the development section, Part III describes contrapuntal techniques, and Part IV is the recapitulation.

The implications of multiple intelligences provide a powerful new argument for strengthening education in and through the arts. In the main, the arts are a celebration of the human spirit; they often present an intracultural sign of the times. In addition to their cultural value, experiences with them are necessary for developing several forms of intelligence and may be equally important in motivating learning on the part of students who do not respond well to traditional teaching.

Readers of this book are urged to form networking alliances on behalf of young people whose basic education will be enriched if they learn to project their spirit into works of art. Our democracy will be immeasurably stronger when it encourages the producers of its future to build upon their own strengths and to choose freely their professions.

Acknowledgments

A conference organizer and book editor could have no better fortune than to have worked with the people whose presentations appear in this book. A friend who managed an artist series once told me that the greater the artist, the fewer the problems. The people whose words you will read presented no problems at all and, what is more surprising, answered my requests by return mail. I am grateful to them.

It was also my good fortune to be assigned Susan Liddicoat as developmental editor for Teachers College Press. Her suggestions have improved the manuscript significantly, and I sincerely appreciate her help.

Part I

THEMATIC MATERIAL

Harold Taylor, in Chapter 1, sets the stage for a consideration of artistic intelligences. A lifetime of rich and varied experiences within the arts and education undergird his perspective of the contemporary scene. He is uniquely qualified to paint a backdrop for discussions of the arts in a democracy and their place in education.

In Chapter 2, Howard Gardner explicates his theory of multiple intelligences, the main theme of the Artistic Intelligences Conference and of this book. He also introduces the two subthemes—implications of the theory for education and methods of implementation.

1

The Arts in a Democracy

Harold Taylor

Roy Blount, Jr., one of our funniest American writers, calls his latest book *Now, Where Were We?* (1988). He says he called it that because it refers to "the end of the Reagan illusion. We're emerging from the past eight years as if we're coming out of a movie theater in the afternoon and blinking in the sunlight and feeling sort of ashamed of where we've just been," Blount explains. "I think it's been an easy decade to be funny about. I think things have gotten so silly that it's hard to make serious sense of them. It seems to be a decade of 'the rich get richer, the poor get poorer, ain't we got fun.' And ain't-we-got-fun-ism is something I don't believe in" (Keep-news, 1989, p. 9).

I agree with Mr. Blount. The past decade has been one of the silliest in our history. But it has been more than silly; it has been dangerously out of control. The possession of money, the accumulation of wealth and expensive objects, the competition for prestige, the obsession with being famous, have resulted in the conception of art as an investment in property and a money-making enterprise. The artist becomes a producer for making objects to be sold to the highest bidder. In an open democracy of the kind we have been developing in the United States, we have now produced a pluralistic society in which greed, avarice, and selfishness are raised to the level of national ideals. We keep telling ourselves that in order to be mentally healthy, we must raise our self-esteem and learn to love ourselves, when what we really need is to do things that command respect and give ourselves some reason for thinking that we deserve to be loved.

We can tell what we admire and value by the amount of money we are prepared to spend: $3 million to pay for a man to hit a ball with a stick, another million or so for a man to run up and down a field with the blown-up skin of a pig under his arm, 40 million more for a lady named Madonna to make a commercial too exciting to be shown to the drinkers of Pepsi Cola, 40 million a year for a man to run a Walt Disney company that is in the art business and find ways of creating fantasy versions of real life, $25,000 for one lecture by a crook from the Watergate scandal, and 25 million for a Jackson Pollock that brought $3,000 to the painter when it was first sold.

We could go on and on with further examples. I haven't even mentioned the military's obscene waste of the national treasury or the stupidity of the redundant B–1 bomber or the airplanes whose sides blew off or the spill of 11 million gallons of crude oil from a ship whose captain lay peacefully in his cabin. The present situation simply illustrates the point we have reached in a pluralistic society powered by money in the hands of corporations. Too few of our citizens have noticed that when one corporation takes over another, it exercises control over a larger and larger segment of the economy and the society itself. Consider, for example, the recent merger of Time and Warner Communications. In one stroke, the boards of directors of two huge companies in the communications industry have taken charge of nearly 20 percent of the American system of communication with more than $10 billion a year in income. In spite of the fact that the publishers are turning out more than 50,000 books a year and authors are now seen in person at public affairs and on television talk shows, you may have noticed that it is almost impossible to find in a local bookstore any book that is not on a best-seller list. Books of poetry are even harder to find.

With the merger of these two giant corporations and the possible merger of others, the Disney Movie Studios, for example, we have the means to consolidate all the arts in one vast corporation under the control of businesspeople who hire their own novelists, writers, dancers, composers, movie and television directors, actors, designers, and producers, and saturate their own media with their own products. One person at a desk in the World Trade Center could control the world's art and entertainment.

The technique of the takeover has also infected the universities at a time when the country so badly needs educational and social leadership. Again, it is a question of money. And lack of moral principle. Consider, for example, the case of the university football and basketball coaches and their presidents, in particular the coach and acting president at the University of Oklahoma. The university had been caught cheating in the awarding of athletic scholarships and in the academic treatment of the athletes themselves. The penalty was three years probation and condemnation by the National Collegiate Athletic Association of the university and its football coach, Barry Switzer, for lack of "supervisory control." Two months after the association acted, five players were arrested. Three were charged with rape; one, with selling cocaine to an FBI agent; and another, with shooting his roommate. When interviewed by CBS, the acting president, David Swank, said, "We probably became a little lax because of the great athletic success we have had, and so we maybe let things slide more than we should." A previous president, George Cross, said at one point that Oklahoma should have a university the football team could be proud of.

AMERICAN WAY
OF SUPPORTING THE ARTS

Athletics and television subsidies are necessary ingredients in the finances of the institutions, and in many ways the athlete sets the tone of the campus social life. He has been chosen to accept the honor of becoming a locally famous public figure, a person of substance whose place in the campus hierarchy is ensured. He becomes part of a social system that includes the fraternities and sororities and their anti-intellectual attributes and habits of mind.

This means that, in large part, there is too little political power in the universities to produce the necessary money from the federal government for support of the arts. In the case of the sciences, few questions are raised on a yearly basis about the necessity of government support of the National Science Foundation. Yet, those of us who believe in the powerful effect of the arts in keeping an open society intellectually and socially healthy are called upon to provide a new reason every year for government support of the arts. A truly democratic political system can be defined, in Lord Moulton's phrase, as "voluntary obedience to the unenforceable," and in the case of the arts in a democracy, there is a natural inclination for all the citizens to have their own opinions about what art is worth supporting. The struggle for the year begins with the usual doom-laden set of remarks about the need for appropriations in other parts of the national budget, and the necessity of cutting the arts budget in favor of more funds for dealing with our social, military, and economic problems.

One of the most effective advocates of government support of the arts is a liberal-minded lawyer named Leonard Garment, who served for five years as cultural consultant to President Nixon and is generally recognized as having been responsible for persuading Nixon to raise the National Endowment for the Arts from a lowly $8 million in 1969 to $75 million in 1974. It is not as generally known that Garment served his apprenticeship in the arts playing jazz clarinet, an art that he still practices.

His advice to the advocates and suppliants is to show the government decision makers what the arts can do and link up the work of the artists and arts people with the educational system. He described what happened to his life when he joined in playing with other musicians in college: "My whole world opened. . . . I had a sense of one of the languages of the world that I would never have had otherwise."

One solution suggests itself when we learn that Belgium, West Germany, Italy, and France, in particular, have all commissioned new works from American dance companies, including Twyla Tharp, Alvin Ailey, and Trisha Brown, and from the post-modern opera group, led by Robert Wilson and Philip Glass, that created *Einstein on the Beach*. Why not have our American theatre, dance, and music supported entirely by the French, who seem more reliable in their response to the idea of subsidizing the arts in America than we do?

In fact, there is a difference between the Europeans and ourselves in our conception of the place of the arts in society. Although we have both fought and won the political battle for democracy, the Europeans have considered the arts to be part of their system of public and social services to be subsidized by the government and made part of the vote-getting apparatus at election time. In the case of the Americans, we have until lately assumed that the arts should be paid for by those who enjoyed them and that actors, dancers, painters, composers, and artists in all other fields should support themselves by the jobs they held or by the objects they sold.

In the years since 1965 when the National Endowment for the Arts was established, the conventional wisdom has deepened to include the realization that the major arts cannot finance themselves by box-office returns plus gifts from corporations and individuals. The endowment awards have increased to a total of $169.1 million for opera, theatre, dance, the visual arts, community projects, folk arts, literature, film, radio and television, music, and museums. Anyone who has gone through the torture of arranging the budgets for ballet and theatre companies will know that $169 million for the huge assortment of arts organizations I have mentioned is only the beginning. The American Ballet Theatre, whose annual budget in the mid-1960s was around $600,000, now has a budget of $20 million; the New York City Ballet costs almost as much. With approximately 250 eligible dance companies applying to the endowment for help, it is clear that even if Congress and the president were united in a passion to support dance, they and the endowment could give only what amounts to a certificate of approval that would make it easier to raise money from other sources.

AMERICAN CREATIVITY IN THE ARTS

At the same time, it is true that the peculiarly American style of practicing an art consists in seizing whatever favorable circumstances are visible and going ahead with them. Andy Warhol came to New York in 1949 at the age of 19 with a fierce ambition that would not be denied. He practiced his art as a commercial artist, drawing shoes and whatever else the assignment called for.

Forty years later he is honored by a show at the Museum of Modern Art of around 300 of his works: paintings, drawings, collages, the famous Brillo boxes and the Campbell's Soup cans, the silkscreen self-portraits, and all the others. He is saying, by the life he led in New York and by his choice and style of subject matter, that anything that attracts attention can be called art. Warhol is a spectacular example of an American artist who not only produced a body of creative work of serious importance for contemporary culture but also managed to invent a public image of himself as famous artist. Robert Frost did the same kind of invention throughout his life.

American dance companies too have sprung into being by the force of the personal character of those who founded them. The two most original and important arts that America has given to the world are the creations of modern dance and American jazz. Both art forms bear the characteristic style of American creativity at its best. That is to say, the dancers make up their own dances with a small group of like-minded companions who are almost completely uninhibited about the movements they invent; the music they either compose themselves, borrow from others, or choose from the taped sound of gurgles, birdcalls, sighs, shouts, noises, or anything else they wish to use.

Each new dance is designed as an experiment in dance theatre (costumes, lighting, stage set); there are no barriers between classical ballet movements by the dancers and the invented, and often improvised, gestures, body movements, and steps of the work in progress. Each company seeks its own audience and financial support and, if successful, establishes itself as a permanent body with its own repertoire.

In the beginning, in the 1930s, for example, Martha Graham was befriended by Ted Shawn, husband and co-worker of the dancer Ruth St. Denis. Graham learned to choreograph and to extend the range of her dancing by taking part in new work with dancers she met through Shawn and St. Denis. Her first extended engagement as a dancer was in New York with the Greenwich Village Follies in 1923. She danced in a number entitled "Three Girls and a Fellow," starring the comedian Joe E. Brown. At the age of 95, Martha Graham still directs her dance company and her school with a worldwide audience and a worldwide influence in the universal vocabulary of dance theatre. It is calculated that there are more than 700 modern dance companies either in colleges and universities or in American communities, and I think it would be safe to say that nearly every one of them shows the Graham influence in some part of its program.

INFLUENCE OF PROGRESSIVE EDUCATION ON THE ARTS

During the 1920s and 1930s, a lively and strong set of ideas was lumped together as the progressive movement, and its major spokesman was the philosopher John Dewey. Out of the ferment of ideas generated in politics and education during those years came the founding of experimental colleges and schools, including Bennington and Sarah Lawrence, where there were no test scores required for admission, no examinations, no required courses, no faculty rank, a self-governing student body, a student curriculum committee for making educational policy, a student council with genuine power to govern, and a curriculum that included theatre, dance, music composition, painting, design, architecture, sculpture, writing, and poetry.

Bennington made arrangements for Martha Graham to hold a summer session in modern dance, beginning in 1934, just at the time that modern dance needed a focal point around which its dancers and choreographers, and particularly Martha Graham, could turn. The Bennington summer school and the work at Sarah Lawrence were more than educational experiments. They were a breeding ground for new ideas in teaching, learning, and creating the arts. They were also invaluable in certifying the legitimacy in the academic community of the place of dance, theatre, music, and the creative arts in the four-year college curriculum. In the experimental colleges, the arts were considered to be a pathway to the enjoyment of life and the development of a rich store of knowledge and experience. In retrospect, it is amusing to recall that the early pioneers in teaching dance in colleges and universities had to sneak the courses into the physical education budget and the athletic departments, and called it "body movement."

A more extreme form of experiment sprang up spontaneously during the progressive years at Black Mountain, in North Carolina, where Andrew Rice, a professor of classics who was fired from Rollins College in Florida for being too ornery and too exciting, brought together a group of dissident faculty members from Rollins and elsewhere. The structure of the program was radically democratic; the concern of the teachers and students for the arts was extraordinarily intense. A talented group assembled there, among them John Cage, Merce Cunningham, Buckminster Fuller, Josef Albers, Robert Rauschenberg, Franz Kline, and Paul Goodman.

The curriculum was made up in impromptu ways by the students and teachers themselves. In some remarks made in an interview in the 1960s, Merce Cunningham explained how the program worked: "The dancers would work every day, and then we would go back to rehearse in the afternoon, and then we would eat and try to lie down, and then we would go back in the evening and rehearse, and when we were exhausted, we would go to bed." The college lasted 23 years, until one day in 1953 Charles Olson, the poet, who had served as rector in the later years, walked out the front door, turned the key in the lock, and left.

IMPETUS FOR EDUCATIONAL REFORM

Although the Black Mountain pattern had no permanence, it had an invigorating effect on everyone who had anything to do with it. It also had a role in serving as a model for the free university movement of the 1960s, when students took over their universities and organized their own curriculum and study-action programs. Those student takeovers were considered dangerous and destructive by most university officials and faculty members. They were looked upon by the students involved in them as the most significant and important experiences of their entire educational history. The students learned how to teach themselves and each other. They learned that academic subjects separated into departmental courses and administered to students in weekly doses by lectures and tests were anti-intellectual and on the whole useless. They learned that theatre, dance, music, poetry, and all the other creative arts, once they entered one's life, had an effect close to magic in giving access to joy and fulfillment.

In other words, if we change the idea about what a college education is for and consider the program of study in college to be an effort to open up the mind and nourish the sensibility and to cultivate what we are calling here artistic intelligences, then we rid the curriculum of what Whitehead calls inert ideas and turn our attention to the ways in which students can become involved in their own education. We will create high schools and colleges of the kind so intelligently constructed as, for example, the North Carolina School of the Arts. Agnes de Mille had a hand in getting the North Carolina project started. With the cooperative support of local educators and citizens, as well as Terry Sanford, then governor of the state, the school in Winston-Salem became a magnet for talented young people not only from North Carolina but from outside the state and from foreign countries. Miss de Mille has found in her own work in developing new ballets that collaboration with educators in the schools and colleges is one of the best ways of helping the country's educational system, as well as helping to create new forms in the arts.

And now for the benediction from the British philosopher, R. G. Collingwood (1938):

> The artist must prophesy not in the sense that he foretells things to come, but in the sense that he tells his audience, at risk of their displeasure, the secrets of their own hearts. His business as an artist is to speak out, to make a clean breast. . . . As spokesman of his community, the secrets he must utter are theirs. The reason why they need him is that no community altogether knows its own heart; and by failing in this knowledge a community deceives itself on the one subject concerning which ignorance means death. . . . Art is the community's medicine for the worst disease of mind, the corruption of consciousness. (p. 336)

References

Blount, R., Jr. (1988). *Now, where were we?* New York: Villard Books.

Collingwood, R. G. (1938). *The principles of art.* London: Oxford University Press.

Keepnews, P. (1989, April 2). Things have gotten silly. *New York Times Book Review,* p. 9.

2

Multiple Intelligences: Implications for Art and Creativity

HOWARD GARDNER

We are coming to the end of the twentieth century. We can begin to look back at a remarkable period in human history, and in particular at the rise of what is now called "modernism" and the "modern sensibility." By introducing certain individuals, I want to recall some of the influential happenings in the first years of the century.

We begin with Albert Einstein. Einstein, of course, remade our notion of how one understands the physical world, replacing the Newtonian synthesis with a more complex relativistic framework.

Next we have Virginia Woolf, one of the principal architects of the modern literary sensibility. In creating a stream-of-consciousness approach, she really helped to shape our notions of the modern novel and modern literature.

Then there is the composer Igor Stravinsky. When *The Rite of Spring* was performed in 1913 in Paris, it ushered in a different view of tonality and also, at the same time, paved the way for completely atonal music in the ears of listeners all over the world. No serious composer after Stravinsky would compose in the same way as before, and audiences heard music in new ways.

What Stravinsky was to music, Pablo Picasso was to the visual arts. Picasso contributed enormously to the modern visual world, in media ranging from painting to film to fashion.

Unlike Harold Taylor (Chapter 1), I have not had the privilege of knowing Martha Graham. But Harold has said what needs to be said

This essay is a transcription of comments made at the opening session of the Artistic Intelligences Conference. It has been edited only in the interest of clarity. The research reported herein has been supported by the Grant Foundation, the Lilly Endowment, the Rockefeller Brothers Fund, the Rockefeller Foundation, the Spencer Foundation, and the Van Leer Foundation.

about the formative role she played not only in modern choreography and modern dance but also in setting up the whole modern dance movement and its institutionalization in this country.

When one thinks about people in the twentieth century who really have contributed to our notions of statesmanship, of diplomacy, of human consciousness, and of human possibilities, Mahatma Gandhi is at the very head of the list.

Finally, I'm a psychologist, so I couldn't really let the opportunity pass without mentioning Sigmund Freud—a psychologist who really has done more to change the way we think about ourselves than any human being in the last 100 years.

Now, having introduced a cavalcade of seven modern masters, I'm first going to ask which of these folks is most important. Most people probably would respond, that's a silly question. I mean, is Einstein more important? Is Gandhi more important? Who's more important, Picasso or Freud? Or are they of equivalent significance?

But let's say I asked, who's smartest? Probably Einstein, right? I mean, Einstein's probably the smartest. But after all, he didn't do very well in school. He failed the entrance examination to a university. Didn't get a job as a professor. Had to work in a patent office. We would say he was a great scientist, but as a violinist he was clearly on the mediocre side. And as a politician, while his heart was on the side of the angels, he was pretty naive. So, Einstein doesn't get a completely unambiguous grade as having been the smartest.

Well, who's smarter? Is it Gandhi, or is it Martha Graham? Is it Freud, or is it Virginia Woolf? Actually—you want to know who the smartest is? The smartest are the members of MENSA, because if you want to get into MENSA you have to have an IQ of 150. And who knows whether Picasso had an IQ of 150? But as far as I can tell, and I hope I do not insult too many people, the major thing that people in MENSA do is congratulate one another on being in MENSA. And that takes time. You know, you have to have meetings, and things like that. Perhaps you wouldn't be able to squeeze in *The Rite of Spring* or the theory of relativity.

I'm trying to suggest that the question of who is smartest isn't a very good question. And by highlighting these various figures who created our contemporary consciousness, I'm trying to suggest that you can't really compare one kind of intelligence with another kind of intelligence. They're *sui generis*. What Freud did is just different from what Stravinsky did.

At the outset I want to explain how we got a certain view of what it is to be smart and what I think is wrong with that view—why I introduced the so-called theory of multiple intelligences. Then I will outline the educational philosophy and practice that might follow from a multiple intelligence point of view and describe some experiments that my colleagues and I have done in schools that serve multiple intelligences—what I call individual-centered schools. Finally I will conclude with a moral to my tale.

CONCEPT OF A SINGLE INTELLIGENCE

Let's go back once again to 1900 when the modern sensibility began. At that time the city fathers in Paris approached a young psychologist named Alfred Binet and said, in effect: "We've got a task for you. Some students are not doing well in school. We'd like to be able to predict which children are going to have problems, and so we'd like for you to make up some kind of instrument that will allow us to essentially winnow out those 'at-risk' youngsters." Binet was quite enterprising. He gave a lot of children a lot of different test items. He saw which items, when passed, predicted school success and which items, when failed, predicted trouble in school. And without knowing it, he had invented the first intelligence (or IQ) test, as we now call it.

Like other Parisian fashions, this one made it across the Atlantic, actually skipped over the Eastern seaboard, and landed in California, where another young psychologist, Lewis Terman, said, in effect, "What a good idea; let's market it." The first normed intelligence test did, indeed, come out of a laboratory at Stanford University, the so-called Stanford Binet test. That was in 1916. In 1917 we went to war. A test called the Army Alpha was given to over a million recruits. We won the war. Psychologists are never hesitant to claim credit for victories, and, in truth, by the 1920s the intelligence test had become very much an accepted part of American life. It was put to many purposes—some of them nefarious, as Stephen Jay Gould (1981) has pointed out. In truth, the IQ test has probably passed its peak as an instrument of use in America. But "IQ-style of thinking" and the kinds of schools that I call "uniform schools," which are also associated with IQ-style thinking, are very entrenched.

In an IQ way of thinking, intelligence can be measured with a short test. Take, for example, the "QT," a test that claims to measure a person's entire intelligence in four or five minutes. Well, Arthur Jensen (1980) says four or five minutes is too long. He puts on a series of lights, the test taker presses a button, and he finds out how smart the person is. Some people still believe in this point of view. Although the IQ tests themselves are not as common as they used to be, the style of thinking is very common.

According to this dispensation, math is most important. Science comes next. Youngsters are tested a lot on their math and science with short-answer instruments. The ones that do the best are called the smartest. They get ahead, do well in school, get to go to the good colleges, and as long as they stay around the university, do just fine. Occasionally, however, some of them walk out into the street. They then discover the import of a whole set of abilities not included in IQ tests.

Uniform schools presuppose some kind of agreement about what's important. Everybody's taught the same thing, pretty much in the same way. All individuals get the same tests, and there's a pretty clear hierarchy of who's the smartest and who's the dumbest. In 1989 many states exhibited more enthusiasm for these kinds of standardized tests than there had been in the past 25 years.

I was not born to be a critic of intelligence tests or IQ-style thinking. I was trained as a developmental psychologist, very much influenced by Piaget, who, I think, is the major figure in my area. And Piaget, as is perhaps not so well known, actually trained in the laboratory of Simon (who worked with Binet), where he learned to give IQ tests. Piaget, in fact, got interested in why children fail, which was a good question to ask; he wanted to unravel the reasoning that led to errors on the IQ test. But Piaget was very much a believer in intelligence as being a single thing. He wrote about 20 books on the development of intelligence (1950, 1982). Some of us had to read them in graduate school. As a student in that era, I believed that, in fact, intelligence all was of a piece, that is, if a person was at one level of understanding, like "formal operations," he or she would be at the same level of understanding with every kind of material dealt with.

That is, in a sense, the heart of the Piaget claim. If a person is concrete operational with one thing, he or she is concrete operational with everything else. And even though Piaget didn't talk much about IQ tests, he basically bought the notion that everybody passes through these stages. Some people pass through them much more quickly, and those people would be the bright people. The people who take more time would be not so bright. Many of us find that what we learned in graduate school has a tendency to stick with us. It's much easier to repeat the lectures you took notes on than to create new ones. I even found that it was easier to write textbooks repeating what I'd been taught in school than it was to come up with my own ideas.

THEORY OF MULTIPLE INTELLIGENCES

In fact, however, the research life that I found myself in every day called to question the very things I had been taught. My research called into question the idea of intelligences as being a single thing that you could measure with a paper-and-pencil test and the idea of all aspects of intelligence being integrally connected in what Piaget would call a "structured whole."

What was this research experience that prompted a change of mind? Basically I worked with two populations. I worked with youngsters, both normal and gifted, at a place called Project Zero at Harvard (Gardner, 1982); and I worked at the Boston veterans' hospital with brain-damaged patients, individuals who were once normal but who had the misfortunes of suffering a stroke that compromised various of their abilities. Every day in working with these populations, I saw things that I simply couldn't explain based on what I had been taught, and, indeed, what I was, myself, preaching. I saw children who would be very strong in one area—it could be language or music or chess or getting along with people—but their strength in one area simply did not predict whether they would be strong in other areas. Some youngsters are good at everything. Some are bad at everything. But most children have very jagged profiles—profiles that are much more complex than the standard intelligence a la Piagetian theory would allow.

It became even more appropriate to challenge these notions once I began to work in a hospital with brain-damaged patients. Now, it could be that if someone had the misfortune of suffering a stroke, all of his or her abilities would decline a bit. Instead of being at 120 horsepower, the person would be at 90 horsepower. But that's exactly what doesn't happen. The location of the lesion is the single most important determinant of what goes wrong and of what stays right. If the damage is in one part of the nervous system, language can break down. In another part of the nervous system, social abilities break down. In another part of the nervous system, musical abilities are compromised. And in each of these cases the other abilities will be spared either entirely or largely.

So, here I was, every day seeing things I couldn't really explain on the basis of what I thought I believed as a researcher and as a writer. Then I got a very interesting opportunity. About 10 years ago, a Dutch foundation called the Van Leer Foundation approached a number of us at the Graduate School of Education at Harvard and said, in effect: "We will give you a grant if you will tell us about the nature and realization of human potential." That's a very big topic. I like to say it's more of a West Coast topic than an East Coast topic.

We accepted the challenge of the Van Leer Foundation to do a study on human potential, and I got an interesting job. I was asked to write a monograph on what had been established in the last few years in the biological and psychological sciences about human cognition. What do we know about the human intellect? About the human mind?

Defining an Intelligence

I decided very early on that this would give me an opportunity—in a sense, a once-in-a-lifetime opportunity—to reflect on what I had observed in human development, in child development, and in the connection or lack of connection between different abilities, and what I had observed in studying patients who had sustained different kinds of brain disease. I would see if I could put these strands together in a more coherent and, frankly, a more generous, more capacious view of the human mind than I had been taught in school. I wanted to construct a broad enough view to encompass the different kinds of things that people around the world can do using their minds. I thought that our view of intelligence was pretty Western-centric—in fact, it goes back to the Greek philosophers.

I became interested, for example, in sailors in the South Seas, who find their way among dozens or even hundreds of islands without a compass, simply by paying attention to a number of cues like the configuration of the stars in the sky, occasional landmarks, and the way the boat feels in water at different degrees of depth. If they had a word for "smart" in the Caroline island chain, they would give it to such sailors because that is what survival depends upon. And whether such a person knew who wrote the *Iliad,* or could count numbers backwards, would not be terribly important for survival there, though when we translate the IQ test into an exotic language, we often expect people to be able to answer just such questions.

I then made what turned out to be fateful decision. I decided to talk not about human talents, which would have been noncontroversial and quickly forgotten, but about "human intelligences." My research effort was an attempt to recognize, identify, and describe different kinds of human intelligences. I did this deliberately, because in a sense I wanted to challenge the people who believe that they own the term *intelligence* and that they alone can determine what tests are appropriate and how that term ought to be used in the wider community.

I define an *intelligence* as an ability to solve problems or to fashion a product, to make something that is valued in at least one culture. Solving problems is noncontroversial. Everybody says if a person is smart, he or she should be able to solve problems. But making something, making a work of art, a poem, a symphony; running an organization; teaching a class—these are uses of intelligence that I'm interested in. Psychologists have had to ignore them because we can't assess those things in four or five minutes, as is the case in the QT. All we can do is to know whether people can answer questions based on "old knowledge." In fact, one of the startling things one discovers in neuropsychology is this: People with frontal lobe disease, who sit like a vegetable all day not engaging in conservation, scarcely eating, never doing anything with their lives, can get an IQ of 140 on a standardized test, because it tests old knowledge and they still have that old knowledge. But it is completely useless. They can't solve any problems except the IQ test problems, and they can't make anything; they just sit there. So the phrase *fashioning a product* throws a real curve to psychologists, as does the last part of my definition—being appreciated in one or more cultures. It takes the focus away from what's important for success in American schools to the much broader question of what it takes to be an effective member of a community that could be very different from ours.

Method of Research

With that as my definition of a human intelligence, I needed a method. What I did was to survey, as systematically as my colleagues and I could, a whole set of literatures that to my knowledge had never really been surveyed before. To the extent that these different literatures all pointed to the same abilities, they gained credibility as potential intelligences. Ultimately I did what I call a subjective factor analysis. I took different literatures, and when they pointed to the same thing, I identified that as a fact, an underlying kind of intelligence. But if something appeared just once and was never mentioned again, or was described very differently in the second literature, then it lost credibility as a candidate for intelligence.

In *Frames of Mind* (1983) I go into quite extended detail about the supporting literatures. I looked at what we know about the development of different abilities in children, both normal and gifted, and which abilities correlate and which ones don't. I took a look at breakdown: When there's damage to the brain system, which kinds of abilities can be counted on to break down together and which ones are disassociated. Those, of course, were the lines of evidence I knew the best, because that's what my work entails.

As to other sources, I also looked at exceptional populations. Prodigies, idiot-savants, autistic individuals, children with learning disabilities—these are all human beings who have very jagged cognitive profiles. Almost no prodigies are good at everything. Most prodigies are good at one or two things and otherwise ordinary. And of course, with autistic children or idiot-savants, it's a much less happy picture. They may be okay in one or two things, but grossly abnormal in others, like Dustin Hoffman's portrayal in the recent movie, *The Rainman*. It is very difficult to explain those individuals using standard intelligence theory, and it's impossible to explain them via Piaget. One of Piaget's principal claims is essentially disconfirmed by every prodigy and every autistic individual.

Let me mention briefly the other sources of evidence: the evolution of cognition across the millennia; cognition in different cultures, like the Puluwat Islands in the Caroline chain where they sail so magnificently; cognition in different species; and two kinds of psychological evidence— correlations among psychometric indices and transfer or generalization from one skill to another. The notion of transfer runs like this: we teach somebody skill area *a,* and we see whether that person gets better in skill area *b.* Transfer is a very old, very entrenched, very appealing concept. At the turn of the century, just about the time Einstein was doing his thing and Binet was doing his thing, psychologists like E. L. Thorndike (1913) were testing the widespread notion that if students studied Latin it would make them reason better, it would make them better in geometry.

Thorndike found that students could study Latin all they liked but it didn't make them any better at reasoning, didn't make them any better in geometry, didn't even make them better in learning Greek (it's not an argument against studying Latin, by the way). In fact, most Latin teachers were quite pleased if pupils were better in learning Latin after they studied Latin for a while. Transfer is very hard to get, and it doesn't happen unless one works at it. I think that there are probably very good evolutionary reasons why. We are trained to behave in certain ways in certain situations and not to inappropriately use those abilities elsewhere because they might land us in big trouble.

I took all this evidence—development and breakdown, special populations, and so forth—and I performed a factor analysis using the computer in my head, and I isolated seven different human intelligences. I make no claims that this is an ultimate list. I claim, instead, that this is a good opening list. If we want to talk about intelligence as being pluralistic, this is a good way to go.

The Seven Intelligences

Now I want to introduce the seven intelligences. Of course, those who are already acquainted with the theory of multiple intelligences will know that the seven people I highlighted in the beginning of my paper each exemplified a different intelligence.

The first intelligence I identified is called linguistic intelligence. Poets have exquisite linguistic intelligence. I once took a course with Robert Lowell, the great American poet. Lowell would take a look at a poem that one of the students had written. He would pick a word that interested him and he would proceed to tell us how every major poet in the English language had used that particular word. His mind was like a cross between the *Oxford English Dictionary* and the *Thesaurus*. I dare say that most people, including me, could spend the rest of our lives reading the *OED* and *Roget's Thesaurus* and we wouldn't be able to do the kind of verbal pyrotechnics that Lowell did effortlessly. He had high linguistic intelligence—as do lawyers, journalists, novelists, and orators.

The second form of intelligence is logical-mathematical—it encompasses the kinds of abilities that logicians, scientists, mathematicians, and programmers have. Piaget thought he was studying all of intelligence, but it is my claim that he was really studying logical-mathematical intelligence.

I mention linguistic and logical-mathematical first, not because I think they have any epistemological or anthological priority. I mention them first because those are the intelligences that are important for standard schools, and even more important for doing well on the standard testing instruments. Individuals with a certain blend of linguistic and logical intelligence will do well on standard tests, and they will be considered very smart.

Musical intelligence is a third form. Stravinsky and Seiji Ozawa, composers and performers—people who can think musically—have high degrees of musical intelligence.

The fourth form of intelligence I call spatial intelligence. Painters like Picasso, chess players, the sailors I described earlier, geometers, surgeons, and architects have high degrees of spatial intelligence. I deliberately mentioned that range of adult roles, because if certain individuals have spatial intelligence, we can't predict whether they are going to become artists or scientists. But if they choose to become artists, we can predict the *kind* of artists they will become. They are more likely to become architects or sculptors than musicians or writers. So intelligences get used (or not used) for artistic ends.

Bodily kinesthetic intelligence, the fifth form, is the ability to use one's whole body—or parts of the body like the hands or mouth—to solve problems or to make things. Athletes, dancers, choreographers, mimes, actors, surgeons again, and craftspeople have high degrees of bodily kinesthetic intelligence.

Finally, I pinpointed two forms of personal intelligence. Interpersonal intelligence is understanding other people. A prime example is an actor, who has to be able to portray the complex relationships among human beings. Those abilities are very important as well for teachers, therapists, salespeople, politicians, and clinicians. Reagan may not have done very well on an IQ test. He probably would have scored lower than Jimmy Carter, but he has an extremely high interpersonal intelligence.

Intrapersonal intelligence is the understanding of oneself—one's own strengths, weaknesses, desires, anxieties, and how to plan one's life based on an accurate model of oneself. It's hard to give an example of intrapersonal intelligence, but I think of a young person reflecting in a notebook—because that kind of activity is one way into intrapersonal intelligence.

Those are the seven intelligences. They represent a point of departure for a more pluralistic view of intellect. Each of these intelligences has sub-intelligences. There are undoubtedly other kinds of intelligences, but I think this is a good beginning to the development of a broader view of this very complicated machine that we have inside our head. It is an insult to that machine to say it can be tested in four or five minutes by measuring how quickly we can press a button. Most of those testers secretly know better, but there's a lot of money to be made in the testing business.

Implications for Artistry and Creativity

What are some of the implications of the theory for artistry and for creativity—these being the subjects of our considerations? I do not believe that any intelligence is inherently artistic or nonartistic. Rather, intelligences singularly or in combination can be put to artistic uses. They can be used to create or to understand artistic works, to work with artistic symbol systems, to create artistic meanings. If I have a high degree of linguistic intelligence, I might become a poet or a novelist or a dramatist, or I might become a lawyer or a journalist. The latter two do not particularly highlight the aesthetic pregnancies in language. One option, one route is not better than the other. It's a certain use. It's an individual choice, and it's a value choice. By the same reasoning, a high degree of spatial intelligence, as I said before, doesn't mean a person is going to become a painter or a sculptor; but it opens up that possibility. The person could decide to use spatial intelligence in that way. It's an individual choice.

I should stress, because I'm often misunderstood about this, that having high intelligence in one area does not necessarily mean that it's the only intelligence important for an art form. In dance, for example, bodily kinesthetic intelligence is important, but so is musical intelligence and spatial intelligence and probably other intelligences as well. One might even be able to be a successful artist using a different set of intelligences than another successful artist. But clearly, those who look exclusively at language and logic are going to miss most of what's important in the arts.

How about creativity? I believe that creativity, like intelligence, is not a single trait; and therefore, as alienated as I am from intelligence tests, I'm even more alienated from creativity tests where people are asked, for example, how many uses they can come up with for a paper clip or a brick. And then they are told how creative they are as if that were the end of this topic. Creativity has a lot more to do with getting to know the subject in great detail, and then being willing to take that knowledge and use it in new kinds of ways; the inclination to use knowledge in new ways is a personality feature and a value feature as much as a cognitive feature.

One particular implication of the theory of multiple intelligences is that people are not creative across the board. People are creative in a domain. In fact, my definition of creativity stipulates the ability to solve problems or to make something or to pose questions regularly in a domain; those questions are initially novel but are eventually accepted in one or more cultures.

So my definition of creativity parallels my definition of intelligence. The important point is that a person is creative *in a domain*. Einstein may have been the most creative physicist of the century, but I've no reason whatsoever to believe that he would have been an equally creative statesman, musician, painter, or dancer. Those involve different intelligences and different domains. And even Leonardo, whom we think of as the ultimate Renaissance man, was probably very creative in areas involving spatial and logical abilities, but there's no particular evidence that he was creative in language, music, or certainly in understanding other people. He apparently was flawed in that regard.

To this point I have provided some background about intelligence and described the major claim of multiple intelligences. Further I have suggested some implications for artistry—how we think about artistic intelligence—and implications for creativity, an area where I think many of our psychological accounts are flawed. What I want to do now is consider some educational implications of the theory.

IMPLICATIONS FOR EDUCATION

The educational implications are quite varied, and they're not at all prescribed. Some people who read my book called up and said, "How about making seven tests for the seven intelligences?"—showing they had really missed the point. Other people said, "What's the school that we should design?" I said, "Look, there are some ideas here. It's not a recipe book." Often when I give workshops, people think I'm going to tell them the five things to do on Monday morning. But I think of the theoretical framework as a set of ideas for people to work with and put to different kinds of uses. Nonetheless, I have acquired some prejudices in the last several years, which I'm going to share.

I begin with two assumptions. One is that not all people have the same minds. In fact, probably each person's mind is different from everyone else's. We look different; we have different personalities; so why should our minds be the same? They're not. We have different and probably changing profiles of intelligences.

The other assumption is that life is short, and my observation is it's getting shorter all the time! We can't learn everything. Probably most of us could work in physics the rest of our lives and wouldn't master all of physics. At a certain point choices need to be made, and I think choices can be either shrewd ones or foolish ones. The twin recognition of the finitude of life and the differences among human minds has led me to think about "individual-centered schooling"; in this form of education, we take extremely seriously the differences among children and try to build an education, an education that in an earlier time would have been called progressive. I make no apologies for a sympathy with progressive education, which makes sense for individual youngsters. I have far less sympathy with the uniform school, where students don't have to wear uniforms, but might just as well because they all must march to exactly the same drummer regardless of their particular set of abilities.

Individual-Centered Schooling

To give you a feeling for individual-centered schools, let me mention the kinds of things that can happen there. Students are regularly assessed, not tested, but assessed in what I call an "intelligence fair way" for their changing profile of abilities. We assess in an intelligence fair way by creating environments in which students can actually show where they have strengths and where they don't. Such assessment must be "intelligence fair." It can't be done through the lens of a paper-and-pencil test, because then what is really being tested is language and logic, plus maybe something else. If we want to determine spatial intelligence, we don't give people a paper-and-pencil test; we put them in downtown Boston and see if they can find their way home. That's a good measure of spatial intelligence.

In individual-centered schools the assessment information is made available to teachers, to students, and to parents. It can be valuable with respect to curricula in two ways. First, with respect to the extent that there are options available, it's fine to suggest to youngsters what sorts of things they might find they have some potential for. But even when you have a mandated curriculum, there is not a reason in the world why everybody has to learn required things in the same way. We might all need to learn history. We might all need to learn geometry. Perhaps we all need to learn Latin, though that's more controversial. But there is no reason in the world why we have to study it in the same way.

As we learn more about human differences in teaching and in learning, and as more interesting kinds of hardware and software and different institutions like children's museums are developed, it's more and more foolish for us to have students sit in a room with a textbook and with a teacher who recognizes only one learning style, and expect everybody's going to learn things in the same way. That's just completely anachronistic. In an individual-centered school, you try to use information about the way people learn—where their strengths lie—to introduce them to subject matters in ways that are appropriate.

In my own case, I had meager spatial intelligence. I would have benefited enormously from access to software programs—ones that could have helped me create with technology the kinds of spatial images I had difficulties conjuring up and manipulating in my own head. Imaginative uses of technology could be instructive for every other intelligence as well.

Finally, this kind of information can be extremely useful for helping individuals find learning opportunities in the wider community. I don't think it's reasonable to expect schools to serve all the intelligences, though I am very impressed by those schools that are making efforts in that direction. But I can't think of any other institution in the culture that can help students find learning opportunities in the community—apprenticeships, mentorships, clubs, interesting kinds of vocations and avocations, learning institutions like museums, media, and so on—that might make a better match for youngsters than does the school curriculum.

Children who have language and logic abilities are going to do fine in school. They're going to think they're smart, and that's going to carry them a long way. If children think they're smart (up to a point, anyway!), that's a very important point in their favor. But not everybody can be smart when there is a single ruler, a single calibration system. We have to try to help all students discover areas where they have some strengths— what I call a crystallizing experience—and to encourage that kind of connection making. We should nourish that: If children find something they're good at and become engaged where they can see progress and where they can find themselves passing from a novice to a more advanced level, that's a tremendously important thing. Not only is it important because it may help them find a vocation or an avocation, but also because it makes them think they have some competence too.

To summarize, those are some ideas of individual-centered schools—

notions about assessment, notions about curriculum choices and teaching and learning approaches, and notions about brokering between students with certain profiles, especially those who are not oriented toward language and logic, and their discovery of a more hospitable learning environment in the community.

Involvement in School Projects

To provide some specific examples of what can be accomplished in individual-centered schools, I want to describe two of the enterprises in which colleagues and I have been engaged in the last several years as a result of our interest in the theory of multiple intelligences. As it happens, these projects range all the way from preschool through high school, but I'm going to focus on the preschool and high school projects in particular.

There is, however, an interesting project at the elementary school level in Indianapolis that I want to mention. Elliot Eisner and I have been working with a school called the Key School, where the staff are really trying to teach to all the intelligences. It's a fascinating experiment, but results will not be conclusive for a long time.

At the preschool level, David Feldman from Tufts and I have a project that we call Spectrum (Malkus, Feldman, & Gardner, 1988), which began as an effort simply to assess different intelligences of young children. It's evolved enormously, and we've created a whole learning environment where youngsters can naturally interact with materials that are supposed to nourish the range of human intelligences—a lot more than seven materials, by the way. In Project Spectrum we are able to "take the temperatures" of these children and see what kinds of strengths they have and what kinds of weaknesses they have, and make concrete suggestions to parents and teachers about what ought to happen with a specific child, given his or her particular configuration of abilities. So, Spectrum began as an assessment, but its entire curricular approach, in many ways, is more similar to a children's museum than to a regular school—though it resembles many decent preschools. In Spectrum, children explore music, the visual arts, dance, the world of the naturalist, the world of the physical experimenter, various kinds of numerical and logical challenges, the realm of taking objects apart and putting them together again, and the like.

Mentioning our so-called "assembly tasks" reminds me of an anecdote I want to relate that is really fascinating. We are working now in Somerville, Massachusetts, which is largely a working class community with many "at-risk" youngsters. In one of the classes where we work, there is a child who at the age of six is already classified as a scholastic loser. Teachers say that he can't do school: "We don't know what he's going to do, but we'll probably have to flunk him," and so on.

As part of Project Spectrum, we gave this child, whom I'll call "Chuck," a set of our assembly tasks. To our amazement Chuck did all of these tasks very easily. He succeeded with one object called the "pump," which no child before had been able to take apart and put together again. We showed a video tape of Chuck's "performance" to two teachers who knew this child—his classroom teacher and another teacher—and his teacher's jaw dropped. Later she told me that she didn't sleep for the next three nights because she was so agitated, but at the same time so stimulated, that a child who she thought was such a loser could do something that she couldn't do herself. She asked how we could create experiences for him in school and outside of school so that he won't become a total loser, because now we know he doesn't have to be.

I want to describe another task in which we use a three-dimensional replica of the classroom for two very different purposes. First, we ask the children to reconstruct the classroom. They love to do this, and it's a rough-and-ready measure of spatial intelligence. Can they put together the classroom the way it is? Some children can do it as well as an adult. And some youngsters can't even tell the long part of the room from the narrow part of the room; they're just completely disoriented.

We also furnish little replicas of the teachers and the children—photographs mounted on little pieces of wood. We ask the children to put together who plays with whom. What do various children do during the day? What does the child himself or herself do during the day? And this set of games around the classroom model serves as a very good, unobtrusive measure of a child's personal intelligences. How observant is the child of other people and of himself or herself?

I hope this demonstrates how by doing things that are just fun for youngsters, we can secure a lot of information about their intellectual profiles. But I want to convey my view that psychologists spend too much time ranking children and not enough time helping them. All of our information in Project Spectrum is fed back to parents and teachers, with concrete suggestions of what might be done given a particular configuration of intelligences.

The last project I want to describe is called ARTS PROPEL (Gardner, 1989). It's a project in middle school and high school being carried out in Pittsburgh with collaboration of the Educational Testing Service (ETS). Whatever disagreements we might have, ETS and our research group at Harvard concur that in the area of the arts and humanities it really makes no sense to use standardized tests. Such multiple-choice instruments are really quite irrelevant. And so we're working in writing, in music, and in the visual arts to create very new "curriculum and assessment vehicles," as we call them.

One vehicle is called the Domain Project. It's like a curriculum module, a very rich set of exercises built around a central concept in the arts; in every Domain Project the children have to produce, perceive, and reflect (PROPEL stands for production, perception, and reflection). In a PROPEL activity, assessment takes place regularly by the child himself or herself, as well as by others; and the assessment occurs throughout the carrying out of this project, not just at the tail end, which is usually the case.

The second curriculum-and-assessment vehicle is called a portfolio, though I, personally, would prefer to call it a processfolio. Most portfolios house final works; in contrast, our processfolios are histories of children's efforts in a project. We document when the project began, what the initial idea was, the various interim drafts, the sketches, the things that are rejected, the things that are valued, what we call pivotal pieces—moments where a breakthrough has been made, collections of the things youngsters like and don't like from the world of great art or pop art, or anything else that captures their interest. And again, though this is more difficult to do with the portfolios than with the domain project, we assess along the way, students as well as the teacher, and then in the end there can be another, more objective kind of assessment.

I have been struck by the enormous difference made by the simple introduction of a portfolio into a classroom. Suddenly things that were ignored or considered unimportant become central. In a sense, what was ground becomes figure, and students begin to look at what they are doing and how they are developing rather than simply worrying about what the teacher is going to think about the final product.

Thus I think we have something powerful there, but I don't want to give the impression that it's our invention. In fact, I'm always amazed that when I get a so-called bright idea, 50 other people in the country are having the same idea. There is a lot of interest in portfolios now, and I think it's salutary, particularly given the mania for testing and uniform schools with which we are surrounded.

CONCLUDING REMARKS

Some people, when they hear what I have to say about multiple intelligences, about individual-centered schools, about domain projects, about portfolios say, "Well, that's all very nice, but who could possibly afford to do it? It's just too expensive, and regretfully we have to go back to uniform schools and standardized tests." To use a technical term, I think that's rot. There is no reason in the world why this nation can't go quite far toward these ideas using current resources. I think the problem is not a problem of resources, but a problem of will and a problem of values.

People have to want to do it. The steps I am recommending have to be consistent with what they think education's about. A lot of the opposition that may pose under the banner of efficiency or economics is really based on a conservative political philosophy about what's important in life and what's important in school.

I said that I was going to conclude with a moral, and I'm obviously getting there. At the beginning of my paper I introduced the concepts of intelligence and creativity by focusing on people who were very important in forming the modern sensibility. And like me, you probably would take your hat off to Virginia Woolf and to Igor Stravinsky and the others. It's very important, however, to point out that intelligence and creativity are not always used benignly. They are value neutral. One can compose for Hitler or paint for Stalin. Einstein's discoveries were put to terribly destructive uses, even as they can be put to uses that are very benign. The same can be said of discoveries about the genetic bases of life. Gandhi and Lenin both had a lot of interpersonal intelligence, but they didn't put it to the same end.

As important as intelligence is and as much as psychologists are interested in it and talk about it, character and vision and responsibility are at least as important—probably more important. How an individual goes about using his or her intelligences within a vision of society is extremely important. As Harold Taylor emphasized in Chapter 1, the arts are a very important part of this consideration. They have been from the time of Plato and Confucius to Pablo Picasso and Pablo Casals. They have not always been used positively, but they have been more often than not.

References

Gardner, H. (1982). *Art, mind, and brain.* New York: Basic Books.

Gardner, H. (1983). *Frames of mind: The theory of multiple intelligences.* New York: Basic Books.

Gardner, H. (1989). Zero-based arts education: An introduction to ARTS PROPEL. *Studies in Art Education, 30* (2), 71–83.

Gould, S. J. (1981). *The mismeasure of man.* New York: Norton Press.

Jensen, A. (1980). *Bias in mental testing.* New York: Free Press.

Malkus, U., Feldman, D., & Gardner, H. (1988). Dimensions of mind in early childhood. In A. Pelligrini (Ed.), *The psychological bases of early education* (pp. 25–38). Chichester, U.K.: Wiley.

Piaget, J. (1950). *The psychology of intelligence.* New York: Harcourt & Brace.

Piaget, J. (1982). *The origins of intelligence in the child.* New York: International Universities Press.

Thorndike, E. L. (1913). *Educational psychology.* New York: Teachers College Press.

Part II

DEVELOPMENT SECTION

As in the development section of a musical composition, the chapters in Part II demonstrate the possibilities of the thematic material. In Chapter 3 Elliot Eisner extrapolates from Gardner's theory of multiple intelligences to the classroom. He writes about implications for education in this country, should the theory be taken seriously, and he presents convincing arguments to do so. Mary Hatwood Futrell, in Chapter 4, reminds us that implementation is a political process, and although politics may be the art of the possible, our goals are too important to be compromised.

Accountability and standardized testing are powerful influences on the schools. The need for accountability is generally accepted, but standardized testing as the means is controversial. Chapter 5 is devoted to testing in the arts, with Howard Gardner and Elliot Eisner responding to a presentation by Warren Newman.

Implementation of methodology resulting from Gardner's theory will move faster if we have models to consider and emulate. It is not easy to effect change in educational policy or curriculum. Cooperative advocacy from significant positions of leadership in the state is necessary, and in Chapter 6 Harriet Keyserling, Charlie G. Williams, and Rose Maree Myers provide a blueprint of actions that have influenced arts education positively in South Carolina.

3

Implications of Artistic Intelligences for Education

ELLIOT W. EISNER

Although Howard Gardner has identified seven types of intelligence, artistic intelligence is not one of them. Despite the omission, Gardner's theory raises some interesting questions: Is artistic intelligence singular or plural? If plural, how do artistic intelligences apply to products of poetry, literature, painting, sculpture, dance, music, and drama? If singular, does it apply to art as a generic process, as one can think about art in the context of science—that is, the doing of science, the doing of math, and so forth? Consider the meaning of the word *art*. Does it refer to a certain quality of experience or to the creation of certain kinds of form? Does it refer to all kinds of products or only to some kinds? It is apparent that there is much work to be done conceptually in thinking about artistic intelligences.

It is also apparent that the idea of multiple and artistic intelligences is more a vision of educational possibility than it is an empirical fact. One of the things that has attracted so many people to the notion is the promise that it holds, its social and educational potential, beyond whether the facts of the case can support the idea. I believe that eventually the facts will support the idea, but what is really attractive to me is that the concept has something to do with the way we lead our lives, the way we run our schools, and how we regard human capacities. I'm attracted by what multiple intelligences might mean for self-actualization.

Although education can be broadly defined, my remarks regarding the implications of artistic intelligences will be focused largely on that social institution we call the school. When one thinks about the implications of artistic intelligences for schools, it seems to me that there are four dimensions that need attention. The first has to do with the aims of edu-

---

This essay is a transcription of comments made at the second session of the Artistic Intelligences Conference. It has been edited only in the interest of clarity.

31

cation. What are we after in the first place? The second implication has to do with decisions about curriculum; the third, with teaching practices; and the fourth, with evaluation. These are four fundamental dimensions of education that are as important for institutions of higher education as they are for grades K–12.

AIMS OF EDUCATION

Cultivating Productive Idiosyncrasy

In considering the first dimension, which requires examining what schools are about and what we ought to be about in schools, it seems to me that one major aim for schools that embrace a view of multiple intelligences is the cultivation of productive idiosyncrasy. To achieve such an aim means providing the conditions through which people become increasingly individuated and increasingly optimized with respect to their unique abilities, the particular talents they possess.

In standard models for the planning of school programs, goals or objectives are to be clearly specified. Once this is done, some procedure, some means, some curricula, some teaching practices are identified that are believed to be instrumental to the achievement of those goals. Next, the curriculum is to be implemented by teachers, and then some evaluation procedure (in our culture a standardized set of achievement tests) is to be used to find out whether the formulated goals have been achieved. The aim of the enterprise is to reduce the discrepancy between the aspirations formulated in the objectives and the behavior or performance of youngsters. The foregoing is a classical planning model. It's recursive. It's a model that epitomizes our conception of what it means to be rational.

The model that emanates from the notion of multiple intelligences is not this traditional model. That is, we are not aiming for everybody to come out at the same place. Uniformity of outcome is not regarded as a major educational virtue. Uniformity is fine in some areas, where there are strong social conventions that youngsters need to learn. In spelling, for example, the least desirable outcome is heterogeneity or creativity in performance. In spelling, it is important for students to conform to social conventions. But aims pertaining to uniformity are usually short-term instrumentalities, compared to substantially more important objectives. And what is substantially more important at the end of an *educational* program, in contrast to a *training* program, is the variance in what youngsters are able to do. Some youngsters are going to do very wonderful things in some areas, but probably not in all areas. In those areas where a particular youngster may not be as able, another youngster will be extremely so.

Heterogeneity among students is the desired outcome—hopefully, productive heterogeneity, or what I've called productive idiosyncrasy.

Let me clarify what I mean with the following illustration. If we put $10 at 10 percent interest in bank account A, and $100 in bank account B, also collecting 10 percent interest, the difference between bank accounts A and B when the money is deposited is $90. What is the difference at the end of the first year? We earned 10 percent on $100, so in account B we have $110, while in the other account we have $11. If we subtract $11 from $110, we get $99. Now we have a $99 difference between bank accounts A and B, whereas at the beginning of the year there was a $90 difference. If we multiply the difference by 12 years, there will be a very large discrepancy between bank accounts A and B.

Now imagine that each student has 60 different bank accounts. If some children come into school with $100 in a particular bank account, and others come into school with $1,000 in that bank account, then over the course of a 12-year program of schooling that optimizes interest rates, we're going to get increased differences among the youngsters. There will also be considerable variability among the 60 different accounts each student has.

The idea this example is intended to illustrate is not trivial. It has important implications for the way we think about schools, because the educational value it promulgates is not convergence to a criterion, but rather, increased variability of outcome. Thus, one important aim of education within the general notion of multiple intelligences is the cultivation of productive differences among youngsters by providing optimal environments for fostering these differences.

Recognizing the Value of
Artistic Representation of Knowledge

A second major consequence of the notion of artistic intelligences for the aims of schooling is the recognition that the creation, transmission, and representation of knowledge are not limited to those propositional forms that are required in the conduct of science. In science, one concludes an inquiry by making claims about the world. What we typically regard as knowledge in our culture is a set of true propositions, that is, claims that are verifiable (or refutable). Science produces propositions that have warrant. Those claims are not expressed in poetry or in pictures. Highlighting nonscientific ways in which knowledge is represented and understanding enlarged is one of the important potential contributions of the idea of multiple intelligences, especially if one teases out its epistemological implications.

In Chapter 2, Gardner described those islanders sitting in a boat, looking at the stars or sensing the depth of the water and knowing where to sail. I used to know a tailor who would put his hand on a piece of cloth and say, "75 percent wool, 5 percent silk, and the rest is linen." He could experience that material in terms of its constituent elements. My point here is that virtually everything people know emanates from the kinds of experience they have. It follows then that the kinds of thinking people are able to engage in are very much related to the kinds of experience they have had. We must come to realize that a propositional discourse, which has been regarded as the quintessential form for knowledge, does not exhaust what it is that people know. Further, propositions do not exhaust what people use in order to acquire knowledge, and propositions certainly do not exhaust what people use to convey what they have come to know. For example, consider literature's contribution to knowledge. People who have forms of linguistic intelligence that are displayed in the use of metaphorical or poetic devices, such as prosody, cadence, and other tropes, are using literary means that help us experience the world in special ways. These kinds of understanding would not be possible if it weren't for those forms. Poetry puts into words, in a certain sense, what words can never say.

Let me say it another way. What makes literature literary? There is a certain kind of form that the writer employs; there is a way in which the language is crafted. An artistic crafting of language requires a special intelligence or combination of intelligences that are necessary for writing literature that informs readers. So we get from Arthur Miller's play *The Death of a Salesman*—from Willie Loman and from Biff and from Willie's wife—a certain kind of experience that tells something about being middle-aged and what it means to lose a job. The point here is that when schools and universities committed to the transmission of knowledge limit knowledge to something that approximates a scientific paradigm, they limit the way people can come to understand. But when we have a more catholic view of knowledge, and particularly the kind that comes out of the arts, we recognize that the avenues to human understanding exceed, widely exceed, what it is that can be said through science alone. There is an epistemic function to different forms of representation. The arts have an extraordinarily important contribution to make to escalating our consciousness, developing our sensibility, and informing us, often empathetically, about what it means to be in somebody else's shoes.

Anybody, or almost anybody, can write about something that's tragic. But to write about it in a way that enables the reader to experience the situation as Willie Loman experienced his is a profound achievement. Art informs us about things that we didn't have the opportunity to experience directly. Therein lies its epistemic function. Thus, one of the important potential benefits of the arts, and it's one that really needs to be teased out, is the more general realization that when we're talking about artistic intelligences, we're talking about ways of knowing. If the mission of the school is defined in terms of knowledge transmission, the arts as well as the sciences, but in different ways, can make a major contribution to the realization of that mission.

CURRICULUM

What are the implications for curriculum? The implications that artistic and multiple intelligences have for the school curriculum lead to double fulcrums for balancing curricula. Those of us who work in education have talked and sometimes still talk about *curricular balance*. The image that comes up is a kind of board balanced upon a fulcrum. I think we need two kinds of balances. One I refer to as a *culturally referenced balance* and the other as a *personally referenced balance*. I do believe that there are fields of study—subject matters—that virtually all youngsters in America should have access to and should learn. There is no question about learning to read, write, and compute; and I don't think there's much question that students should learn something about the history of the world and of this country, about some aspects of science, and so on. All youngsters need to become culturally literate, but they also need to have opportunities in schools to pursue certain areas in depth for which they have particular proclivities. What I am referring to here is a personally referenced curricular balance, one that provides the conditions through which, to use Joseph Campbell's phrase, "youngsters can follow their bliss." Their bliss may be what it is that they can do really well, where they can come into their own. If a youngster is really interested in doing scientific work, that youngster ought to have opportunities to work with other people in science in an immersed way, in a way that generally is not now provided in ordinary classrooms. So we have to have it both ways. Schools have a general social mission in which there are certain generic materials that youngsters ought to have access to as part of becoming citizens. But at the same time, schools ought to be places where youngsters can follow their bliss, develop their proclivities, and foster their intelligences—the ones they have the inclination to pursue.

Allocation of Time

Of course, to make this happen, we have to be willing to devote that most precious resource in our schools and in our lives—time. In fact, if we want to determine the educational priorities of a school, the worst place to look is in the district-wide syllabus that tells about the district's goals. The best place to look is at how the school allocates time.

The allocation of time is crucial, and it does not have to be allocated in terms of the conventional unit, that is, 40 weeks to a subject matter. The way we honor this tradition, you would think that it came down to us from Mount Sinai. The school I attended 40 years ago had the same structure and features as schools today. School started in September and ended in June. If a course was taught, it started in September and it ended in June. I graduated and went to a university that was organized to teach in quarters. Although uniformity is a convenient organizational device, it is not one that is essentially educational.

There are two issues here. One is, how much time is devoted to what? If we calculate the number of units of time assigned to a subject, we'll get an operational definition of educational value. Then there is something called prime time. In 90 percent of the elementary schools in this country, when the arts are taught, they're taught in the afternoon and often near the end of the week. That's not prime time. Because there is such a bifurcation of cognition and affect in our educational theories, we plan for students to think in the morning and to feel in the afternoon. We teach what they need to "think" about in the morning and the things they don't really have to "think" about in the afternoon. The time slot assigned to a subject and the amount of time that's allocated to it through the curriculum reflect our priorities. If we take seriously the idea of multiple intelligences for schooling (and it's easier not to take it seriously), there are implications for the way we allocate our most precious resource—how we choose to spend our time.

Nongraded Schools

Another far-reaching implication of multiple intelligences is that schools should move to nongraded structures. Since variability within and between students is to be optimized, and since graded schools tend to suppress variability (the graded school as an organizational convenience was developed in 1859 in Quincy, Massachusetts), we have to do something else with a body of content other than assign it to a grade level. The grade continues from September to June. The students are tested in June. If they know the contents of the grade, they are promoted to the next. If they don't know the contents, they are retained. And if they know the contents for the grade ahead, then sometimes they are double promoted. That's the logic; it's tidy, systematic, and organizationally convenient.

But children do not develop in tidy patterns. The range of reading achievement in a nonselective heterogeneous class is approximately equal to the grade level itself: At the first grade there is a one-year range; at the second grade, a two-year range; at the fifth grade, a five-year range; and at the seventh grade, a seven-year range of reading achievement. A fifth-grade teacher who is teaching only fifth-grade reading is missing those who are beyond or below the fifth grade. What we have is an organizational structure laid on youngsters whose personal development does not parallel the way in which the school has been organized. But we have another problem as well: Parents want to know what grade their child is in—a social expectation that creates still another kind of issue and presents another kind of constraint.

TEACHING PRACTICES

What are the implications of artistic intelligences for teaching? Teaching, if we take the notion of artistic intelligences seriously, would employ a wide variety of forms of representation so that students could play to their individual strengths. Consider, for example, a teacher trying to help students understand the slavery period prior to the Civil War. How do we help youngsters understand something about the life of slaves in the 1850s? One way to do it is to ask them to read a textbook that addresses this topic. There are many such textbook assignments given in schools. But there are many other resources a teacher could draw upon as well. There is the music that was created and the dances performed by slaves. There is the kind of food that was eaten. There are films that could be shown (*Roots*, for example, which was on television a few years ago). There is the folksay that was created—the myths and stories retold. In other words, what we try to do when we take multiple or artistic intelligences seriously is to broaden the array of resources that are brought to bear on topics students study. Varied resources that provide different kinds of opportunities for youngsters with different proclivities (different intelligences) enable them to secure forms of understanding that would not be available without those resources.

In other words, the diversification of resources broadens the opportunities that youngsters have for understanding the subject matter. Since different resources make different kinds of understanding possible, as long as schools operate on an essentially linguistic modality that gives place of privilege to a kind of literal, logical, or mathematical form of intelligence, schools limit what youngsters can learn. They also impede youngsters whose intelligences are in modalities other than the ones that are emphasized. In broadening the resources through which the material can be grasped—regardless of the subject area—the probability that youngsters will learn is likely to increase.

The basic idea here is not to put every youngster through the same narrow eye of the needle; when we limit the game to basketball, children who are three-foot-two are going to be handicapped (speaking metaphorically). When we diversify the resources that youngsters can use to understand a historical period, we create a greater sense of cognitive equity for youngsters and broaden what they can learn. I think that Toshiba, Apple, and IBM understand this very well. One of the major selling points of the computers they produce is the way that visuals are provided, the colors that are used, and so on. It is increasingly being realized that the way in which information is displayed affects what can be learned. These resources are not simply vehicles for gussying up the computer so that it is a more attractive item to sell; these computer displays enable people to understand things that otherwise would be lost. Multiple intelligences need multiple resources for nourishment.

EVALUATION

Commensurability

What are the implications of multiple and artistic intelligences for evaluation? In schools that embrace the theory of multiple intelligences, students would be afforded opportunities to display what they've learned by using forms of representation that play to their proclivities. Evaluation is both a very complicated issue and a very interesting one. We live in a meritocracy, and we are very much interested in matters of commensurability. Most university admissions committees use indices like GRE scores to make judgments about individuals. They take transcripts and convert grades into GPAs; they look at high school transcripts and at SATs. One of the functions of these resources, as they're handled mathematically, is to convert uniqueness to some common standard that makes it possible to make comparisons. In fact, the normal distribution is a device through which people are sorted out. That's what an IQ score tells us. Because it's in a normal distribution, if we know somebody's IQ score, we know what percentile that individual is in. Consider an IQ score of 116; if we know that the normal distribution has a 16-point standard deviation, we can determine the percentage of people who are below 116. The ability to make such comparisons has to do with commensurability.

Commensurability requires that people be provided with the same task so that comparisons of their performance can be made. I've been sitting on the Stanford School of Education Admissions Committee for 23 years and have found GRE scores to be the easiest and the most seductive data we use in making judgments about human competence. Even though we know that only the upper and lower scores tell you much, we look at all of them. We get excited when we see a 700 verbal on the GRE, even though it doesn't say anything about whether that person has creative ideas or is motivated or intellectually interesting. My point is that in a meritocracy when we're trying to identify who's on top and who's below, we want to have information that's displayed on a common scale. However, when we take seriously the notion that there really are differences among students in the kinds of intelligences they operate with and we also take this notion seriously in our evaluation practices, we are going to have to give youngsters opportunities to represent what they have come to know in very different ways, regardless of whether it exacerbates the problem of commensurability.

In fact, that is exactly what happens in life. Three people take a trip to Jerusalem. One is a writer, one is a painter, and the third is a poet. The writer writes, the painter paints, the poet creates a poem, and all three products might be fine. Saul Bellow wrote *To Jerusalem and Back*. I have been there, too. I don't know that he sees more than I. Maybe he does, maybe he doesn't, but he writes better than I do. So he gets published, and I don't even write about it. The issue here is that people use different forms of representation to render the situations they experience. The social utility of those differences is that they inform us in a variety of ways. What I can get from a Saul Bellow novel about Jerusalem is not what I can get from a painting of the same city—or a poem or a dance, or from a sociological study, or from some mathematical representation. If you've got classrooms that are introducing students to the Civil War through different forms of representation, then evaluation data should also come in different forms.

Such a practice is likely to distress evaluators and test makers because when diverse data are provided, commensurability becomes difficult to achieve. But if commensurability is not what we're after in evaluation, that is, if we're no longer trying to sort people on the same scale but, instead, trying to evaluate the qualities and differences in their understanding, we encounter a new type of technical problem. To cope with this problem requires a very different evaluation model from the ones we now use; the appropriate evaluation orientation calls for looking at differences both within and between students.

Portfolios

We have to pay attention in our assessment not simply to where a youngster is in a distribution, but to where that youngster has come from on a variety of dimensions. That, of course, is one of the great utilities of portfolios, or *processfolios,* as Gardner explained in Chapter 2. They are a diachronic record indicating where youngsters have been, and that's important. Instead of just looking at one point, we can look at a trend.

Using portfolios for assessment also allows firsthand examination of the data. When we look at test scores, we've transformed the particular and reduced it to a number, but when we look at a portfolio and see paintings, the data are there, so to speak. The individuality is there. If you rated paintings and said, on a 20-point scale, this one's a 10, that one's a 9, that one's an 11, and this one is a 5, you wouldn't have the data. You'd have symbols. In a portfolio we've got the data, whether they are written samples, visual samples, or mathematical samples. We're really close to the phenomena rather than to their reduced symbolic representation.

With a new model, we would provide people with opportunities to represent what they learned from courses in forms that are not necessarily congruent with the forms the subject matter took when the learning occurred. This approach to teaching, learning, and evaluation needs to be played out; it will have important consequences for the way we think about assessment.

The implications of this idea for universities are also important because those who manage the universities' gates create a ripple that goes right down to the preschools. If universities acknowledged the various culturally important differences that youngsters going through school possess, admission criteria would be broadened considerably. At Stanford and at most other institutions, student applicants send in their transcripts, and calculations are made. In this process, the admissions office does not factor in grades that students received in art or in music or in dance. Those grades are set aside. So here is the irony of an institution that gives a B.A., an M.A., and a Ph.D. in art and in music on its own campus but won't consider grades in the arts for students wishing admission.

Consider the SAT, which is given to about 1,750,000 high school seniors each year. There are only two columns reporting performance—verbal and mathematical. I've always suggested that there should be a third column—competence in lute playing. If we had such a column, we would have such a run on lutes that we'd have to import them from China. Lute playing would be taught in upper middle class neighborhoods first; we might even have preschool lute. Those who keep the gates to higher education significantly influence the priorities of the schools below them. If universities took the idea of multiple intelligences seriously, it would have an effect not only on who gets in, but also on how elementary, middle, and secondary schools operate.

CONCLUSION

The major implications of multiple and artistic intelligences could revolutionize educational policy and practice in the 108,000 schools in the United States. Good schools, in this view, would aim to diversify the outcomes of schooling; they wouldn't seek to make outcomes uniform. They would seek to cultivate productive idiosyncrasy by increasing variance, rather than attenuating it. We wouldn't think about schools as operating an assembly line of learning, which is the way we have thought about schools in this country. The language of education is very much an assembly-line language. Every 6,000 miles we "in-service" teachers, we "install" programs, we "align" curricula—curricular alignment, program installation, in-servicing!

School curricula would become more equitable by providing, as it were, different strokes for different folks. Equity requires diversity. Sameness is not the same as equity. It is not equitable for someone who is five-foot-one in high school to have basketball as the only athletic game available. In other words, if basketball is the only game in town, a youngster who is terrific at soccer is going to be, so to speak, handicapped. Schools embracing the idea of multiple intelligences would have a different conception of equity.

Teaching would utilize multiple forms of representation to foster learning and would develop the ability to "read" forms other than those that are linguistic or mathematical.

The implications of these ideas are structural, they are procedural, they pertain to curricular matters, and they pertain to matters of teaching. We can talk all we want to, but when we're playing marbles for keeps, we've got to think about the concrete implications of taking this notion seriously.

Plato put it nicely a long time ago. He said, "What is honored in a country will be cultivated there." New aims of the kind that we've been talking about will require a new infrastructure—new curricula, new pedagogy—and, as I suggested, new approaches to educational evaluation. We will need to develop new conceptual models that are more attractive than the ones that we now have.

Finally, let me end with a word of caution about multiple and artistic intelligences. There is the possibility that in our desire to acknowledge different intelligences, we may develop a deterministic attitude toward them. Although most people don't think about it that way, the school curriculum is fundamentally a mind-altering device. It's a device for changing minds, changing the way people think. Moreover, schools are not just for changing the way people think, but for improving the way people think. We need therefore to exploit the power of the curriculum to optimize whatever potential intelligences individuals possess. Further, we must remember that there is at least one important lesson that the study of culture teaches—different cultures prize and develop different cognitive abilities. The environment shapes the curriculum.

We need to be careful about adopting a view that, after recognizing the presence of multiple intelligences, proceeds to develop individual profiles of these intelligences; thus creating a self-fulfilling prophesy that reinforces certain abilities (intelligences) but somehow neglects the development of the others. There is a need to look at where those proclivities are, but not necessarily to assume that the initial profile is fixed or that no attention needs to be paid to those areas in which a youngster may not display a high level of intelligence at a particular time. The factorial constancy of different intelligences is something that needs to be determined; in the effort, we don't want to back into a new kind of determinism.

On the whole, I believe multiple intelligences is an idea that has significant potential for helping us rethink and support what we conceive of as the proper mission of education. It will take much more than enthusiasm for this idea to make it work. It will take careful attention conceptually, technically, and politically to the major educational institution we have in our country—our schools—to change those well-entrenched practices with which we are all too familiar. We have a big job ahead of us, but one that is worth doing.

In closing, I want to mention something that I feel very proud about: Those of us who have worked in arts education have been way ahead of the game on this one. It really does my heart good to observe some of our most able cognitive psychologists discovering the cognitive dimensions of the arts. I sometimes imagine myself standing on that seashore in Gardner's Puluwat Islands, and they are out there, rowing in these boats, coming nearer to us. Come on! Come on! We've been waiting for you. What has taken you so long?

4

The Challenge of Implementation

Mary Hatwood Futrell

At the outset, I want to confess that I am not, by any stretch of the imagination, an artist. I am not a curator. And, quite frankly, I cannot even be called a connoisseur of the arts. I first visited a museum, first attended an opera, and first heard a live symphony performance as a college undergraduate. So I'm still catching up. And I have a long way to go. I am still at a point where my "political literacy" outdistances my artistic literacy. I think I do know, however, a little bit about the politics of education.

I bring the perspective of one more familiar with a world much less sublime than the world of art, a world lacking in elegance and harmony, a world, to get to the point, that's sometimes downright ugly. But this world—the political world—is, despite its absence of beauty, a world that we ignore at our peril. For if we do not shape the political world, the political world will shape us.

My remarks, then, rest on the premise that only political savvy of the highest order can ensure that the theory of artistic intelligences advanced by Howard Gardner will become a vibrant force in America's classrooms rather than a musty relic in university archives. The challenge confronted by the education community in securing a central place for the arts within the K–12 curriculum and in altering the status quo so as to ensure that education unleashes rather than stifles the potential of students possessed of artistic intelligence, is as much political as pedagogical. It is from this perspective that I wish to outline the challenges I believe must be met if the implementation of the theory of artistic intelligences is to become more than a wish, more than a hope.

REJECTING AN APPEAL TO ECONOMIC UTILITY

The first challenge, perhaps the most fundamental challenge, is to reject (in both word and deed) the temptation of instant gratification. Let

43

me explain this rather strange assertion. All of us in the education community have been too often tempted and too often seduced by strategies that, in the long run, intensified rather than eradicated the ills we sought to cure. For this reason, I think we would all be well advised to commit to memory H. L. Mencken's observation that "to every complex problem, there corresponds a simple solution . . . which is invariably wrong."

The simple solution now within reach is a direct result of the present economic and political climate in the United States. Given this climate, the assumption within much of the education community is that any discipline, any instructional strategy, any reform initiative, any bold theory, can best be defended by establishing its economic utility. In other words, we increasingly tend to assume that we must defend ourselves, our instincts, our prized projects, by demonstrating that our agenda is critical to the cause of America's economic resurgence.

This is, in my view, a prime example of a strategy that will produce short-term ecstasy and long-term agony. What now seems clear is that, if we elevate the arts to new prominence by defining their value solely, or even primarily, in terms of the economic crisis America now confronts, if we make the case that artistic intelligence is a neglected weapon in an economic war that has reached crisis proportions, then we face the very real danger that when the economic crisis passes, so too will the day in the sun for arts education.

Prestige quickly acquired is prestige quickly lost. Our colleagues who teach foreign languages have learned this lesson the hard way. In 1957, the National Defense Education Act, passed by Congress in response to the launch of Sputnik, diverted massive funds to the cause of improving and expanding foreign language instruction. But as soon as America's own space program got off the ground, so to speak, the funds dried up and interest in foreign languages languished.

A similar sequence followed the Arab oil embargo in the early 1970s. And today, foreign language teachers at all levels of American education confront the very real possibility that this scenario will once again be repeated. Economic adversity and the challenges of the global economy have again spurred interest in foreign languages. The latest crisis of the hour (precipitated by economic developments in the Pacific rim, in Western Europe, and in the Soviet Union) has given new prestige to foreign language study. Will this interest prove long lasting? History tells us it will not. When our economic crisis passes, foreign languages will in all likelihood once again become neglected orphans.

If other disciplines are to avoid this kind of periodic setback, they must reject overly narrow views of the mission of education. Today, that requires defeating the mentality that defines education as of strictly utilitarian value, as an instrument of economic conquest. This is no small task. Indeed, it may require something on the order of a social revolution. But leading that revolution, or at least actively advancing it, further defines the first challenge that must be met. For today, the future of arts education is at risk. And the reason it is at risk can perhaps best be explained by examining the discourse that today dominates the dialogue on education reform. The vocabulary, the buzz words, in that debate are very revealing.

Today, we are told with increasing regularity that knowledge is a commodity, education an industry, learning an asset, research an enterprise. We are told, in effect, that the business of education is business. Personally, I don't feel that any philosophy so deeply rooted in the thinking of Calvin Coolidge will serve us well. For us, as educators, to take our bearings from Calvin Coolidge strikes me as comparable to taking lessons on the public responsibility of elected officials from Richard Nixon, or defending collective bargaining by appealing to the wisdom of Frank Lorenzo. In short, I do not believe that our national self-interest will be well served (nor do I believe that artistic intelligences will receive due recognition) so long as we take it as a given that the purpose of education is to ensure that Fords and Chryslers outsell Toyotas and Nissans.

My advice, then, is this: If Gardner's theory of artistic intelligences is to have an impact, it must first be established that arts education is critical to the cause of meaningful, quality education. But arts educators cannot accomplish this task by depicting themselves as economic warriors, first, because that claim, to be perfectly frank, lacks credibility, and second, because an appeal to the utility of art will, in the long run, serve them poorly. In fact, this appeal will serve education in general poorly.

Let me explain. In the last five years, new and imposing challenges to America's preeminence within the international marketplace generated a new national consensus. For the first time in years, education was seen not as the problem, but as the solution; not as the cause of U.S. economic decline, but as the agent of U.S. economic renewal.

This consensus soon solidified, and American corporate leaders were saying what education leaders had been saying for years, that an undereducated America cannot remain competitive in the new world economy. The president of IBM began to sound at least a bit like the president of NEA. Candidates who wished to serve in the White House echoed the belief of those who serve in the schoolhouse, that America's might does not reside in silos packed with missiles but in young minds packed with potential.

America now understood, at long last, that education is the engine that drives our economy and sustains our democracy. Unfortunately, this principle became inverted. What we were soon being told was that the economy ought to be the engine that drives education. That's not acceptable. It's not healthy. I submit that we must never permit a single interest to define the mission of education. I further submit that if we do, there will be a price to pay. And part of that price will be the exile of the arts to the margins of the curriculum. In fact, that may be a best-case scenario. The greater threat is that the arts will not merely be confined to the margins, but will be moved off the page entirely.

The challenge confronting us (and it is a major challenge) is to affirm the importance of education as an instrumental value while also insisting that our curricula must reserve space for those academic pursuits that have primarily intrinsic value. If we fail in this mission, if we are politically ineffective, if we are unable to sway public opinion and influence policy makers, we will find ourselves worshipping at the altar of corporate priorities. And if that happens, we will have sacrificed far too much that is far too valuable to the well-being of our students, to the cause of educational excellence, to the future of America, and to the quest for a more secure, more just world order.

ENHANCING THE VALUE OF THE ARTS

But if an appeal to economic utilitarianism is, as I am insisting, unwise, then how can the arts survive this age that is so deeply absorbed in the issues of trade balances and deficits and stock market fluctuations? What will ensure that the arts acquire the esteem they deserve? What will ensure that artistic intelligences will acquire equal footing with technological intelligence? What will ensure the survival of the principle that man does not live by bread, or by technology, alone? And what will ensure permanent respect for the knowledge that finds expression in poetry and painting, in drama and dance, in music and mime and architecture and photography and sculpture?

These are, to be sure, imposing questions. But in raising them, I can't help but remember another of H. L. Mencken's observations: "Some problems are so difficult that they can't be solved in a million years, unless someone thinks about them for five minutes." So I do have an answer, though arriving at it, I admit, took more than five minutes. My answer is threefold. But this triad is unified by, it is animated by, a single conviction, which Martin Luther King, Jr. expressed in a speech during his senior year at Morehouse College: "Education which stops with efficiency may prove to be the greatest menace to society. Intelligence is not enough. Intelligence plus character, that is the true goal of education." My conviction, then, is that if we are to survive the difficult final days of this difficult century, we must become a people who give as much thought to standards as to the stock market, as much thought to morality as to technology, as much thought to ethics as to economics, as much thought to artistic beauty as to economic utility.

Today, that goal is so distant that it's barely visible. But I remain confident that we can arrive at it, and I'm convinced that an artistic renaissance is a fundamental prerequisite for successful completion of the journey. Let me outline the route.

Art as a Civilizing Influence

First, I believe that we can learn something of value from E. D. Hirsch (1988), something that takes us beyond the exercises in trivial pursuit that constitute the heart of his teachings on cultural literacy. Hirsch has observed:

> Today, more than in any earlier time in our history, purely utilitarian aims happen to coincide with the highest humanistic and civic purposes of schooling, purposes such as promoting a more just and harmonious society, creating an informed citizenry, and teaching our children to appreciate the worlds of nature, culture, and history. (p. 17)

The conclusion I draw from Hirsch's insight is that economic adversity has generated a rare opportunity. That opportunity is the result of what we might term, to borrow an old phrase, a "trickle-down effect." The economic imperative for a work force that can carry us through the twenty-first century has created an imperative for global understanding, which in turn has created an imperative for arts education as a force that fosters cross-cultural understanding. In brief, economic adversity has taught us that the study of art, and artistic expression itself, is not a luxury but rather a necessity.

The most recent report from the National Endowment for the Arts, entitled *Toward Civilization* (1988), makes precisely this point. Unfortunately, this document does not give adequate emphasis to art as a civilizing influence, an influence that can help us understand that the ideals that unite the peoples of the world are far more important than the differences that divide them.

Art as a civilizing influence, art as a source of the self-understanding that refines our capacity for understanding the neighbors with whom we share this planet—this, I believe, is the case we must take to the American people. This is the message we must carry to our communities. This is the message we must see that Congress hears. And this is the message we need to promulgate at every college and university that prepares the teachers who will prepare the students of tomorrow for life within our shrunken world.

Art as Essential to Global Understanding

If this crusade is to succeed (and this brings me to the second part of my three-part answer), the intellectual climate within our nation must shift. For this reason, I suggest that, as we attempt to foster respect for the world of art and ensure pedagogical responsiveness to artistic intelligences, we would be well advised to pay heed to, and to resuscitate, the teachings of classical Greek philosophy.

I am thinking in particular of Pythagoras. For Pythagoras might be characterized as a radical interdisciplinarian. It was Pythagoras who insisted that the most intimate of all disciplines are mathematics and music. Yes, music, which, for Pythagoras, was clearly among the basics. I think of this often when I hear the "back-to-basics" advocates define the arts (and music in particular) as educational frills. No one who accepts the imperative for understanding other cultures can accept this categorization.

Music is among the keys that open world history and offer us access to the souls of civilizations past and civilizations still in the making. It is the language of the emotions—not raw emotion, but emotion rendered articulate, emotion corralled by intellect. Anyone who understands the difference between cacophony and a symphony has begun to understand the meaning of civilization, the meaning of the quest to wrench order from chaos. In the present age, I know of no more valuable lesson.

Similar statements could be made about sculpture and painting, about literature and dance and architecture. These are the windows to cultures and nations that seem alien. As such, they are, to borrow the fashionable cliché, windows of opportunity. Those windows must remain open, for through them flows the air that awakens and sustains global understanding.

Art as a Focus of Teacher Preparation

Let me now move to the last part of my three-part answer for how to ensure that artistic intelligences receive their due. This will necessitate a leap from the sublime world of ancient Athens to the somewhat less sublime world of modern academia.

If we are to meet the needs of tomorrow's adults, then we must recognize, and act on the recognition, that all aspiring teachers must have the ability to prepare students for the world of tomorrow, the world emerging today. These students will be part of a world in which their competitors, their colleagues, and their brothers and sisters will live not only in New York and California and Tennessee, but in Zurich and Paris, in Tokyo and Nairobi and Moscow. They all must help bring harmony to a world that for too long has known only discord.

If future teachers are to have what it takes to prepare students for this new world, I know of nothing that can help them more than intensive study in the arts. What I am suggesting is that the future of global studies and of artistic intelligences may depend decisively on restructuring teacher preparation programs. I will not elaborate on this suggestion, but I will add that I think this issue deserves the concentrated attention of artists, art historians, art researchers, and art instructors at every educational level. Based on my own experience, I have no doubt that teacher education has nothing to lose and everything to gain if it grants a privileged position to those disciplines whose subject is the human spirit and whose goal is the ennoblement of that spirit.

EDUCATING FOR WORLD PEACE

At the same time, I know that focusing on art as a prerequisite for the civic and social demands of tomorrow still defines art as primarily an instrumental value and only secondarily an intrinsic value. I will try, in the remainder of my remarks, to remedy this defect in my comments. I'll begin by sharing the observations of Delwin A. Roy (1989), president of the Hitachi Foundation. Roy notes that our rhetoric about global understanding has not been matched by deeds. He then asks why this is so, and answers his own question.

> Much of the failure lies in the negative way the challenge has been posed. . . . We have been enjoined to adopt new attitudes, . . . but primarily as a way to defend ourselves from foreign competitors. This is the rhetoric of fear; these are scare tactics. Such rhetoric does not truthfully portray what's wrong, what we must do, and why. . . . The real challenge is to be the most constructive world power we can be.

Let me build on this valuable commentary: I submit that our present attitudes toward peace and national security are the residue of attitudes that may have been appropriate in the era prior to World War II. They are not appropriate today. Today, we must understand that national security is inseparable from international security, that no nation can be free of fear as long as one nation is engulfed by fear, that no part of our planet will know peace until every part of our planet knows peace. That is why our national interests need not blind us to the common interests we share with all nations and all peoples. Those interests can become inseparable, and that inseparability can bring peace.

The prerequisite for global peace is global understanding, global understanding that arises not from fear, but from hope, from a sense of the oneness of the human family that, throughout the ages, art has done so much to promote. The global understanding that will move us beyond fear and beyond belligerence demands an education that recognizes a principle higher than the profit motive and nobler than economic conquest. Art will of necessity have a central place within any such education, and artistic intelligences will hold a lofty and respected position. True global understanding demands an education that drives home the message that, to borrow the words of President John F. Kennedy in a speech given on June 10, 1963, at American University, "in the final analysis our most basic link is that we all inhabit this planet. We all breathe the same air. We all cherish our children's future. And we are all mortal."

The advocates of an educational system that gives these principles equal footing with economic imperatives need not apologize to anyone. For our commitment is to the young people of America, and to the young people of the world, to the students of today who will be the guardians of all our tomorrows. We must prepare those students not merely for acquisitiveness but for inquisitiveness, not merely for a world dominated by technological advancement but for a world elevated by artistic achievement. I appeal to educators throughout the nation to help move America toward this goal.

The day that goal becomes a reality will be a day to be welcomed. For on that day, we will have helped move America, not toward dominance, but toward prominence, prominence as a nation that solidified its security by giving its children the gift of understanding other children. That's a day when pride will be justified, a day when we will be able to say that we had the courage to so thoroughly transform learning that we secured for our children safe passage through the twilight of this often dark century, a day we will be able to say that we—we, the people—gave life to the principle that I believe can and must guide every educator, the well-known principle that we do not inherit the world from our ancestors, we borrow the world from our children.

That principle is, I submit, sheer poetry. May such poetry guide us. For the power of poetry, more than the power of weaponry, may just ensure the survival of our planet. Artistry, more than militancy, can give new meaning to an ideal as old as the scriptures and as compelling as the morning headlines, the ideal of peace on earth, good will toward men. And active artistic intelligences, more than strategic defense initiatives, offer the best hope that the forces of civilization will hold in check the forces of barbarism. And, in the process, save us from ourselves. And save for our children a world of beauty, a world of harmony.

References

Hirsch, E. D. (1988, January). Cultural literacy: Let's get specific. *Issues '88: A Special Edition of NEA Today,* pp. 17–42.

National Endowment for the Arts. (1988). *Toward civilization: A report on arts education.* Washington, DC: U.S. Government Printing Office.

Roy, D. A. (1989, May). *What is the Pacific Basin's approach to philanthropy?* Paper presented at the meeting of the Foundation for Independent Higher Education, Palm Springs, CA.

5

The Effect of Standardized Testing on Education in the Arts

WARREN BENNETT NEWMAN

When I received the assigned title for my paper, I was both chagrined and pleased. Although this topic is not necessarily very exotic, for us at the National Endowment for the Arts it has turned out to be possibly one of the more controversial aspects of some recommendations that we made in the report *Toward Civilization* (1988), which we were mandated to give to Congress and the president about one year ago.

The report explicitly stated that it was the position of the National Endowment for the Arts and the Arts in Education Program to support assessment and testing and evaluation in the arts. I will elaborate a bit on that recommendation further into the discussion, but here let me indicate that what I particularly liked about the title for this paper was its singular emphasis on the effect of standardized testing in the arts. When I thought about what concentrating solely on effect meant, I decided that this could be a very short paper because we don't have standardized testing in the arts; therefore, there is no effect!

PROMOTING THE VALUE OF THE ARTS

That we don't have testing in the arts does speak a great deal. It says something about what we value and how we show what we value. Based on this vacuum, one could conclude that we don't value the arts.

In discussing standardized testing, let me personalize the issue by re-turning to my days as a teacher—how different education is today from when I started 33 years ago. At that time, we did not have regular stan-dardized testing as we know it today. Testing was not a political issue because when we did have testing, we didn't pay much attention to it. We gave the test according to administrative protocol, and our students followed the procedures. When we got the results back, we looked them over. Although we got different kinds of reports—which were not too sophisticated—we did virtually nothing with them. In those days, testing really didn't hurt us too much because nothing politically was done with the results. This is to say, they were never printed in the newspaper for the world to see. Parents didn't know much about them, and frankly, neither did the staff. I know that I didn't discriminate between how we dealt with individual student scores and how the school system dealt with school and district scores. Standardized testing in those days did not affect what teachers did in the classrooms. I am particularly reminded of this when I hear the current discussion about teacher empowerment and professional enfranchisement. I believe that I was more enfranchised as a teacher in 1956 than many teachers feel they are today, particularly when it came to making curricular decisions in terms of what I felt was best for my students. I honestly believe that I was more accountable then than I would be under the current vogue of accountability. Testing has become the major mode of establishing accountability, as well as examining course offerings, dropout rates, and other factors. In too many cases, I think that cause is confused with effect, input is viewed as more important than output, and means are not separated from ends. Testing has become enmeshed in the often contradictory crosscurrents one finds in today's schools.

We at the Endowment recognize that a part of our agenda is process and a part is product; the former is political, the latter pedagogical. In political considerations of education today, if a subject is not tested in the curriculum, it is not considered of value. We want to use whatever means appropriate to make the arts important; testing is one strategy for doing so. And if testing is part of the accountability movement, we want the best testing program possible. In today's climate, that means group standardized testing as well as individual assessing. Testing itself is not the problem. The quality of our testing and our understanding of its limitations are the problems. When it comes to testing and accountability, ignorance is not blissful. While some educators may understand the limitations of standardized testing, there are many teachers, administrators, board members, legislators, and community persons who do not. They do not know enough about the psychometric properties of standardized tests, or even criterion-referenced tests, to be in control of the results from such testing.

Let me illustrate with a story of ignorance about testing. I remember dealing with a board of education in the 1960s in relation to a proposed state law that would have based every child's promotion to the next grade level upon his or her scoring above the mean on standardized tests in core curriculum areas. In spite of the absurdity of such an approach, there were people who thought that the law was needed. In order to help the board members understand the problem, we took an hour at a board meeting and gave them a short, fairly easy test and then showed them how the mean was determined. Then we let them take the test again and improve their performance. Alas, they saw that, by definition, half of them would always fall below the mean, regardless of how well each or all of them did on subsequent tests.

Another problem we have with testing involves semantics. We use norm-referenced, standardized, and criterion-referenced adjectives to describe different types of testing. In addition, we use assessment and evaluation to describe different aspects of accountability-related issues. Many people who are opposed to standardized testing often accept criterion-referenced testing without criticism, or at least with the same level of criticism as they do norm-referenced testing. Furthermore, good teachers already know what students know when it comes to the content of "little" tests. Much of the criterion-referenced testing is based upon little and often unimportant mini-units of work, particularly in reading, math, and language. While the reliability of such testing may be high, I question its validity. But more important, I think criterion-referenced tests are often a waste of time, giving a false sense of accountability. My own view is that all testing and assessment is normative in the sense that every act of judging or comparing something with a standard is normative in terms of what we expect as either predictable or desirable performance. Quantitative objectivity has very little to do with it.

There are a variety of reasons why the Endowment has taken a very strong position on testing specifically as well as assessment in the more general sense. The Endowment's position is basically that arts education is important for all students, not just the talented and gifted. Otherwise, we cannot be assured that we will have a culturally educated, literate citizenry. Given the multicultural nation that we have become in this small, multicultural world, the arts are a necessity, not a luxury. It is not enough to instruct; we need to know how effective the instruction is. It is just as important in the arts as in the sciences to measure the degree of learning by students. These issues—the place of the arts in the curriculum and the current concern about accountability—provide the basis for my support of testing, including standardized testing, in the arts.

USING THE ARTS TO IMPROVE
THE QUALITY OF TESTING

Having said that our position is to use testing as leverage to make the arts more important than they are perceived to be now, we recognize that there is the danger that poor tests will be used or that good tests could be misused. We don't want to repeat the errors found in testing other curricular areas.

However, we do think that using the arts themselves may, in fact, help to improve the quality of testing. For example, the portfolio assessment approach as described by Gardner in Chapter 2 deals with validity without the liabilities incurred in group testing. But we have to recognize, as Eisner pointed out in Chapter 3, that schools do have a dual responsibility in terms of the individual student and the society at large. Aside from the skills involved in the creation of art products, we have to ensure that students know about their culture, their society, their history, and all of humankind's history. What we can't seem to agree on is specifically what it is we want them to know. In a practical sense, until we solve that problem, we cannot create the best testing instruments. I hypothesize, however, that by addressing the standardized testing issue in the arts head on, we will clarify knowledge questions.

There are ways we can take current means of assessment and use them as the basis for developing more traditional test instruments. For example, I remember working with a third-grade teacher who was against testing. We began our venture by agreeing that it was important for her students to know about balance in terms of symmetry and asymmetry. During the course of the year, she instructed her students on the concept and devised ways to help them learn the concept. The assessment process used at the end of the year was the creation of a flower arrangement. Students had a variety of vases, flower cuttings, and greenery from which to choose. They could work individually or in small groups of two or three. They had to make decisions on the nature of the arrangement they would create, its balance, the size, texture, and color of vase and flowers—the aesthetics of the product, if you will. Then they had to present their work to the rest of the class, hear the criticism, and consider ways in which they could improve their art product. In essence, we were interested in the control that students had over their creation. Instruction could then go on to the kind of re-creation of still life works that artists of the past and present have created, leading from the base experience in the classroom to that found in galleries and museums.

What we, the teacher and I, began to consider was how some of the learning that had obviously taken place through this process could be tested. Unfortunately, I came to Washington about that time, so I couldn't continue on the project. I do think that this story illustrates one way to begin the construction of tests in the arts from an experiential base, not just a theoretical one.

LEARNING ABOUT THE ARTS
THROUGH TESTING

Just because we don't have good instruments today with which to test the arts, doesn't mean that we should not have a policy that is explicit and positive regarding testing in the arts. Testing in the arts should reflect all the uses to which we put the art. What are those uses? The arts present the natural world to us in ways that help us to appreciate its beauty along with its awesomeness and mystery. The arts offer ways of bringing order, rules, rituals, and repetition to life. The arts help emphasize or clarify the meaning of life at several levels of understanding. To what degree could we test these concepts and see how peoples at various times in history have used the arts in shaping their individual and societal lives? The arts help prepare us for the unexpected and the unfamiliar; are those ideas and behaviors that can be tested? The arts help us to be selective, nonhabitual—an area of challenge for testing. What do we see that is not normally seen or hear that is not normally heard? Could we, in fact, help children hear silence through testing? Art has therapeutic value in terms of the personal interpretation that we give to arts experiences and the resultant catharsis, when that occurs. Gardner (Chapter 2) discussed the social ends of arts. Are those concepts not testable along with the formal elements of the various art forms?

I think testing in the arts may tell us something about the arts themselves. Are there aspects of the arts that inherently make learning about them difficult? Testing might help answer this question.

Finally, I think that if we did a good job of testing in the arts, we could get beyond the tyranny of the categorization of the arts so that students could see not only what is unique in each art form but what is common, how the arts transcend their own forms to become a part of generic life experiences for all people—that the sensory modes are the ways in which human beings communicate, and that over time human beings merge and create new forms of expression. What testing could help do is to make the arts seen as the core of human experience and understanding.

Standardized testing is a political necessity and an educational opportunity. Although the current state of testing the arts is deficient, there are strong arguments for improving its present and future use.

Response to Newman's Presentation

Howard Gardner

Warren Newman has been very gracious and also very moderate sounding, so I may appear ungracious and immoderate as I take issue with some of what he says. We have to realize that Newman is speaking, in a sense, from his position in government. Therefore, he doesn't have as much latitude as somebody like me or like Elliot Eisner, whose positions are only self-imposed. I believe that Newman is "trying out" his position. We should all be allowed to do that, and I could certainly try out a position in favor of testing in the arts. We should recognize, however, that he is tentative, trying on a position for size, so to speak.

The reason that I don't resonate to it does not mean that I am against assessment; I'm very much in favor of assessment. I think it's something every growing organism, as well as every relatively mature organism, should be doing regularly, naturally, almost reflexively. It should become a part of the way we think, write, and work. Assessment is a natural and important aspect of any kind of professional growth. I also have nothing against rigor, nor do I oppose a notion of standardization per se. My real quarrel is with testing, not assessment, and with the unavoidable connotations that it has nowadays. Testing is the word that we apply to de-contextualized instruments—measures devised elsewhere—which are brought in at prescribed times. Usually students answer with pencil and paper, then the responses are sent away, and a score comes back to tell them how good or how bad they are.

Nowhere did Newman say this was the kind of thing we ought to be doing. Yet, I think it is inevitable that when someone takes a position in favor of standardized testing, as he did, most people think it means testing basic skills, administering the SAT, and so on. In fact, the use of standardized tests answers a need that legislators and school board members think they have, but it does not answer the needs of youngsters.

If Newman had taken this position 30 years ago, I think it would have been much more viable. As he said, 30 years ago standardized tests were given irregularly and weren't taken terribly seriously; one could have wondered about their effectiveness and whether they should be taken seriously. I heard it pointed out recently that in the 1950s the average person took about two standardized tests in his or her entire life. Nowadays, every child who goes to school takes dozens, if not hundreds, of tests. Yet nobody would seriously claim that our education has gotten significantly better over the last 30 years. In fact, scores on the College Board Entrance Examinations indicate that it's gotten worse.

Why then do I think that the position Newman is taking is no longer tenable? It is the same reason that Elliot Eisner alluded to at the end of Chapter 3—cognitive psychologists are finally realizing that what they've thought about assessment is not the last word. Over the past few months, each of the New England states, except for Massachusetts, interestingly enough, has approached us at Harvard Project Zero to say, in effect, "Will you help us with doing portfolio kinds of assessments?" That's a staggering thing because nobody would have said that even five years ago. Furthermore, my associates and I have been asked to develop portfolio-type assessments in science and math. The kinds of evaluation in which the arts are taking the lead are now being followed in other areas of the curriculum; Newman made this same kind of comment.

Thus, if I were in his shoes, I think that I would be taking the position that we should be concerned about assessment. We should be worrying about what students are learning, and we should be worrying a great deal about what kinds of things we are requiring them to learn (and whether the arts are included and whether they are included in an appropriate way). But we should also be very, very suspicious of the technology and the thinking that, in a sense, has made psychometrics into an enormous business; in fact, it's a business that is much more successful for the stockholders than it is for the clients—by whom I mean the teachers and the students. I think that associations like the National Endowment for the Arts and the Department of Education in particular ought to be promoting alternative, more qualitative, more context-rich, more on-sight kinds of assessments and evaluations.

I had an opportunity to testify to the National Commission on Testing and Public Policy (1990), which is funded by the Ford Foundation. Interestingly, over half the people on that commission are lawyers. I think it provides some insight into what issues about testing really are. I said to those people that over the past decade, billions of dollars have been spent on standardized testing. If we throw some more money at this enterprise, it's not going to get significantly better. Basically, we've gone about as far as we can with number-two pencils and multiple-choice tests. What we ought to be doing is spending some millions on new forms of assessment, much more qualitative forms of assessment, things that pay attention, as Eisner said, to the individual aspects of what children do. There are too many proven disadvantages to the present system. I think that the National Endowment for the Arts should keep its portfolio (and now I'm using portfolio in another sense) very much intact for the support of alternatives to standardized testing.

Response to Newman's Presentation

ELLIOT W. EISNER

My comments may indicate that Howard Gardner and I have some disagreements. I have spent a major portion of my career developing qualitative approaches to educational evaluation. I'm very much interested in looking at classrooms with the kinds of lenses that critics apply to works of art—to movies, to dance, to the theatre, and so forth—as a way of really getting at the phenomena I care about. I want language that is nonquantitative to be used to display what goes on in schools and classrooms so that the understanding of what transpires is a lot richer, more detailed, and more replete than what one gets by simply looking at test scores. Having said that, I want to complicate the matter because in a discussion of testing, we need to avoid oversimplification.

Tests are shorthand devices for getting information about human performance. They typically are decontextualized, as Gardner suggested. That is to say, they are constructed by a teacher or a testing service as a resource for evoking a response of one kind or another from which judgments about performance can be made. In the United States, however, there is a whole range of functions that different forms of assessment or evaluation, including testing, can perform.

Insofar as schools have social responsibilities that are common (the dimension of the curriculum that I described in Chapter 3 as being culturally referenced), I think there are legitimate common expectations about the knowledge that youngsters should be helped to acquire and understand. Teachers are usually obligated to teach in schools that serve a wide variety of students, and I think that it is misleading to look only at those dimensions of schooling that are assessed by standardized tests. But at the same time, I think that it is important for us to find out what schools are accomplishing. In the arts, an overabundance of standardized tests "ain't our problem"; there are about nine tests listed in *Tests in Print III* (1983), most of which were developed over 25 years ago.

The National Assessment of Educational Progress (NAEP) was supposed to assess the arts. They did so in 1974–75 and again in 1978–79 and haven't done it since. The NAEP employs a multiple-matrix approach to assessment. What that means is that they don't give all students all test items. They give individual students a sample of items, and they are not interested in the performance of any particular student, or even the performance of any group within a school district; they are interested in the general picture of student performance within a region of the country for a particular age group. In other words, NAEP takes the educational pulse of an area of the nation. This pulse might be represented by the following illustrations: If students who live in Colorado don't know where Denver is, I think we ought to know about it. If students cannot identify the United States on a map of the world, I think we ought to know about it. I'm not pushing such knowledge as the *sine qua non* of education—there are things more important than Denver or even the location of the United States. But I'm trying to get at the issue that I think Newman was alluding to: There are some wide-ranging social responsibilities that motivate testing (and he was very careful to recognize publicly that there are potential downsides, including the coercive effect that testing has).

What can we find out through testing a large population that will reflect what students actually know? Last year when I was speaking to the Philosophy of Education Society, I was trying to make a point about genre in art, and I mentioned Umberto Boccioni. From the lack of response I perceived in the audience, I decided to ask, "How many of you know who Boccioni is?" Three hands went up. I said, "Now wait a second. How many have heard of futurism?" A few more. I was checking for understanding. I was trying to get some information as to where my listeners were. If I talk about Boccioni and they've never heard of him, and if I talk about futurism and they've never heard of it, then as a teacher I've got a whole lot of other things to explain in order to speak meaningfully. My checking for understanding in that lecture is a small version of checking for understanding in a region or nation. It can be very useful.

In part, the problem is how do we learn what we ought to know about understanding on the part of large populations, except through standardized testing. Even though testing doesn't provide a whole lot of diagnostic information immediately, it does provide some survey information that is not irrelevant for revealing what schools are accomplishing. At the same time, we must also use the kind of custom-made, contextualized assessments that have a great deal of instrumental utility in the educational process. Any time a teacher asks a group of youngsters or an individual to engage in some kind of activity, there is a type of experiment taking place from which an assessment can be made. When a teacher raises a question, that is both a test and a kind of experiment. Does the youngster understand? Are the youngsters responding?

What Gardner is advocating, which I think is very important, is that situated, contextualized tasks have the potential to provide a lot of information about how students are doing. Teacher-made tests, which are somewhat less contextualized than what I've just described but more contextualized than what the national assessment provides, can also furnish teachers with useful feedback about their students' performance, which can be taken into account in dealing with curricular matters. Thus, the problem is getting a wide-ranging consensus on meeting our social responsibilities, then getting a sense of whether students have learned some important ideas, and finally doing all of this without allowing the evaluation process to manage the system. At the same time we should be doing the kind of fine-grained, closed-circuit observation and assessment that provides teachers and parents with what they need to know about how their particular students and children are doing.

I'm trying to get across the idea that when you look at assessment problems in education, they exist at several levels because tests serve different purposes. Professional responsibility should keep us from jumping too quickly on bandwagons that don't go much deeper than slogans.

We need to examine the complexities and study the subtle differences that have been briefly mentioned, but here I can only adumbrate the issues, the varieties of assessment, and the potential functions that they can perform. Yes, we now use standardized achievement tests that too often take the options out of teachers' hands, and we publish the results in a local newspaper without an iota of interpretation; assessment can drive the system, but that's not why we test. We need to develop the kind of assessment that will help us know where youngsters are with respect to certain general aspects of education. At the same time we need to develop assessment methods that focus upon individuals. We need both types—and more.

Newman is extremely mindful of the political issues involved, but he and I and other educators are not happy about what we have provided so far in our schools in the way of arts education. If we can get some leverage through standardized tests, I think it may be a good thing *as long as we don't give up our souls in the effort*. It's a delicate problem, and I invite everyone to participate in the dilemma-like considerations in dealing with it. To deal with it well, we will need to initiate responsible, professional deliberation among colleagues from all the arts.

References

Mitchell, J. V., Jr. (Ed.). (1983). *Tests in print III*. Buros Institute of Mental Measurement, University of Nebraska–Lincoln. Lincoln: University of Nebraska Press.

National Commission on Testing and Public Policy. (1990). *From Gatekeeper to Gateway: Transforming Testing in America*. Boston: Author.

National Endowment for the Arts. (1988). *Toward civilization: A report on arts education*. Washington, DC: U.S. Government Printing Office.

6 IMPLEMENTATION: SOUTH CAROLINA MODELS

The Politics of Mainstreaming Arts in Education

HARRIET KEYSERLING

It is fitting that a conference that is focusing on a new and exciting concept in education and the arts is taking place in South Carolina because in recent years this state has become a national model in educational reforms, and we are also a national model in active partnerships between the state legislature and the cultural community. That is what I'm going to discuss: the politics of mainstreaming arts in education, as well as in other facets of state government.

The Joint Legislative Committee on Cultural Affairs, which I chair, was created by the legislature in 1986 and is one of just a few such committees in the country. It was an outgrowth of a Governor's Task Force on the Arts, created by Governor Dick Riley three years earlier. The Task Force's mission was to examine what was going on in the arts in our state and to make recommendations to encourage and expand arts and cultural activities in both the public and the private sectors, encouraging as much cooperation among all players as possible. This Task Force consisted of four legislators, representatives of the governor and the lieutenant governor, and the chairpersons or directors of state agencies that were, or should have been, involved in our state's cultural programs. These included the powerful (as state agencies go) Development Board; the Parks, Recreation, and Tourism agency; Educational Television, as well as representatives of K–12 and higher education; and, of course, the basic cultural agencies (the State Library, the State Museum, the Archives and History agency, the Arts Commission, and the Governor's School for the the Arts Commission, and the Governor's School for the Arts).

The Task Force put in place a coalition that enabled the arts community and a few legislators like me to expand and move the arts forward at a surprising rate, for a relatively poor state not particularly perceived as a center of culture in the country.

To go back in time a little: Before I came to the legislature 13 years ago, I spent a lot of time struggling to keep alive a variety of arts activities in the small town of Beaufort, South Carolina. Other than several pleasant encounters with the state Arts Commission, I had little knowledge about the arts across the state; you might say the visibility was low for the arts.

When I came to the legislature, I didn't know how much support for the arts there was among other legislators and didn't ask, because I assumed that with so many needs in our state, there was not a high priority for funding the arts. I was lucky enough to be appointed to a national legislative committee on the arts, which had just been created with legislators from every state participating. I discovered during the process of sharing experiences (legislators love to compare their states and share experiences) that there were things that the state government can do that don't necessarily cost a lot of money. But even more important, I discovered that there were very persuasive arguments available to sell the arts, to show that they are a good investment and that they are important not only for their intrinsic value but also for stimulating economic development and tourism, two goals almost every legislator, in every legislature, is working for.

But how to get this word out? By somehow developing a coalition of advocates with credible, even establishment, credentials. I talked with Governor Riley, who shared my enthusiasm for the arts, and he created the Governor's Task Force on the Arts. I must admit that I didn't consciously think, "Now we must build an infrastructure for the arts." I was really groping around, looking for allies in the legislature and in state government offices who would support the arts and the programs of the Arts Commission.

The Task Force found that more cultural activity existed than we had expected. But we found little cohesion among the players. We spent several years touting the relationship between cultural vibrancy, quality education, and economic development; but, more important, we brought the cultural community into the mainstream of South Carolina's government and business community. In 1986, we were successful in replacing the unfunded Task Force with a funded joint legislative committee. The Task Force had existed, year to year, by the grace of the governor; the Joint Legislative Committee on Cultural Affairs was written into law. Not only did this institutionalize culture in the legislature (very important in a state where the legislature is the seat of power), but now there are five House members and five senators actively involved in cultural issues.

I must admit again that this also was not part of any skillfully laid plan. It came about one day as we were debating the Appropriations Bill on the floor of the House when a member of the Task Force, a much more optimistic and aggressive person than I, ambled up to me and said, "Why don't we put money in the budget for a legislative committee on the arts?" This is not the usual procedure. But we talked to some Ways and Means members, and they agreed not to oppose such a move, possibly because I was a Ways and Means member and it is a custom to yield to members' requests if not too outrageous, or possibly because our request was very modest—we asked for only one not-very-well-paid staff person. Probably they agreed because of the visibility the Task Force had brought to the arts, as well as the links we had forged with the power structure of the state.

Our committee's official mandate is to coordinate and increase cooperation among all agencies involved in cultural affairs, to analyze the roles of government and the private sector in supporting the arts and cultural resources of the state, and to develop alternative approaches to supporting the arts. We make recommendations for programs, legislation, and the use of resources of state agencies, including education, in the promotion and enhancement of the arts.

The Joint Legislative Committee on Cultural Affairs, along with the state Arts Commission, forms the base of a *cultural infrastructure*. We network with all of our state's core cultural agencies, with whom we meet regularly to exchange ideas, to share information, and to help each other with projects.

We also network with the state Development Board and relentlessly remind them that recruiting and retaining major industry in South Carolina depends on the quality of life that our state offers. And that quality of life is dependent on the vibrancy of our state's cultural industry. In partnership with the Arts Commission, we commissioned the University of South Carolina to do a study of the economic impact of the cultural industry in South Carolina. We joined forces to help the Spoleto Festival, a shining example of the positive impact that cultural activity can have on a city. Those who have been to Charleston recently will know what I mean. We also work with our Educational Television Commission and the state Department of Education.

We collaborate with the Governor's School for the Arts, another model South Carolina offers the country. Established in 1980 by Governor Riley, this five-week residential honors program, under the leadership of Virginia Uldrick, offers intensive study and artistic enrichment in the summer to rising juniors and seniors who possess exceptional aptitude in creative writing, visual arts, theatre, music, and dance.

An important aspect of the school is the master-apprentice philosophy, which allows students to study with master artists-teachers. Students receive both group and individualized instruction from a distinguished faculty and nationally renowned professional guest artists.

The success of the Governor's School has been impressive. Since the first session in 1981, enrollment has grown from 118 to 250 students. Additionally, a two-week dance program was initiated in 1988 for younger dancers. The school's outreach program seeks to identify artistically gifted students from rural areas and assists them in applying more successfully for admission to the school.

In addition, the Governor's School offers a graduate studies program for outstanding teachers in arts education from across the state. Our education reform package, which I will mention later, included funding for tuition reimbursement for teachers accepted into this program. As these teachers return to their own classrooms with new techniques and skills for meeting the needs of artistically gifted students, school systems throughout South Carolina will benefit from the program.

Let me narrow the focus now on how our legislature has worked to support arts in education, efforts that have culminated in another of South Carolina's model projects, the Arts in Basic Curriculum (ABC) plan. I want to describe, step by step, the combined efforts of the South Carolina General Assembly, the South Carolina Arts Commission, and the state Department of Education to bring arts in education to all students in South Carolina, not just the gifted and talented. This plan would not exist if it had not been for the total cooperation between these state agencies and the legislature.

The story begins in 1977, and I am pleased to point out that the level of cooperation and support from the General Assembly has increased steadily. In that year, the South Carolina legislature passed the Education Finance Act, an effort to equalize education across the state. Included in the act was funding for art and music teachers and a defined minimum requirement of one certified art/music specialist per 800 elementary students. This laid the groundwork for further programs that have been the product of a committed and able state Arts Commission, working with committed and able arts educators, starting at the top with the state Department of Education (under the leadership of Charlie Williams) and spreading down to administrators and teachers in the field.

All of these people not only work very hard at their jobs but have built as sophisticated and successful an advocacy, a grass-roots lobby, as any I have seen. Unlike industry, they have no money to spend on entertaining or hiring professional lobbyists. They do it themselves, joining with the local arts councils and interested parents. They are all important elements of our cultural infrastructure and have a great impact on the legislators.

In 1984, the nationally acclaimed Education Improvement Act (EIA) was passed in South Carolina. It set in place bold initiatives that directly affect the quality of education and create a statewide awareness of the importance of investing in education. Funding for the academically and artistically gifted and talented was included.

When the initial funding for the artistically gifted was threatened in committee, a strong grass-roots lobbying effort kept it in place. When the new governor (who must have been unaware of how strong public support was) vetoed those funds out of the budget, another lobbying effort was set in place, and the funds were restored the following year. There has been no attempt since then to dislodge them.

In 1986, our Cultural Affairs Committee initiated, with the help of the Arts Commission and the state Department of Education, a comprehensive statewide survey of arts education in all South Carolina public schools. The survey was completed in 1987. The recommendation of the volunteer advisory committee for the survey was that a comprehensive arts education should be provided for every child in South Carolina.

Also in 1987, the Arts Commission initiated its "Canvass of the People." These are regional meetings across the state that serve as public forums on the arts. Arts in education was a major topic at every meeting. Educators, artists, and arts councils testified to the need to provide a comprehensive arts education for all students if South Carolina is to have a healthy arts environment, stable arts organizations, a climate where artists can make a living, and, most important, well-rounded citizens. Members of the Cultural Affairs Committee participated in meetings in their districts, a very good consciousness-raising education for them. These forums led the Arts Commission to take a leadership role in advocating for arts in education.

In March 1987, based on the input from the Arts Commission's Canvass meetings and the Cultural Affairs Committee's survey and recommendations, the Arts Commission applied for and received a planning grant from the National Endowment for the Arts. South Carolina was one of 16 states to receive such a grant. With the grant funds, an ABC Steering Committee was appointed and began to develop a plan to incorporate arts into the basic curriculum. It will also serve as an oversight body during the implementation of the plan.

This committee is a wonderful, inclusive coalition of arts education leadership throughout South Carolina. The Cultural Affairs Committee also participates in this group, and its largest contribution probably is providing political advice. Scott Sanders, Director of the Arts Commission and a fast learner, showed great political acumen by asking a legislator, Representative Joseph H. Nesbitt, to chair the committee. He is a member of the House Education Committee, which also handles cultural legislation.

The ABC Steering Committee worked in tandem with the Arts Commission and the state Department of Education to develop the plan, which was submitted to the National Endowment for the Arts in the spring of 1988. The National Endowment ranked South Carolina's plan number one in the country and awarded our Arts Commission an implementation grant.

In 1989, in order to keep up the momentum of our educational reform movement, a Blue Ribbon Committee was appointed to develop an additional reform package. Some call it Son of EIA. The ABC Steering Committee urged the Blue Ribbon Committee to insert the ABC plan into their recommendations. With the assistance of Rep. Nesbitt, the ABC proposal was built into the new education legislation. At this time, although the legislation has not yet passed, the funding—$600,000—has already been put into the Appropriations Bill by the Ways and Means Committee and passed by the House. (It did not hurt that four of the members of the Cultural Affairs Committee are on Ways and Means.) We are hoping that the Senate will not tamper with this money and that the House and Senate will approve the pending legislation this year.[1]

The ABC project is an exciting and innovative model program that should serve as an example to other states in many areas. In the area of interagency cooperation, we doubt that the plan could have been formulated without the state Department of Education and the Arts Commission working together. And, obviously, legislative support every step of the way was enormously helpful.

South Carolina is once again in the national forefront, this time in arts education. It has been exciting to be a part of the collaborative effort of the legislators, art educators, the Arts Commission, parents, and even the industry leaders who have made it all happen. We will try to keep the coalition intact and work together on new and challenging projects in the future.

I hope you found some or all that I have described of interest, even of use, to you. If South Carolina, once at the bottom of the education totem pole, can produce such model programs, so can other states.

---

1. The final appropriation for the 1989–90 fiscal year was $360,000.

It's Time for the Grandchildren to Study the Arts

CHARLIE G. WILLIAMS

I have taken my title from a statement attributed to John Adams, who said that his generation studied war and government, in order that the next generation might study commerce and agriculture, so that his grandchildren might study the arts. I particularly appreciate President Adams' vision, even though it didn't happen in that sequence, and I doubt seriously that we will get to the point where we will no longer, as a society, have to study government and war. I think, however, that in South Carolina we are having a renaissance of interest in the arts, while we are still concerned with commerce, agriculture, government, and national defense. We have a new sensitivity and a new awareness that general arts instruction should be provided for every child in public schools and nonpublic schools as well.

In addition there should be a special effort to develop the unique talents that children have. We have been about that effort since we mandated that the arts be taught, and not only taught, but taught by certified, trained individuals. In my own early experiences in public education in this state, I can remember when the music program of a school consisted of a person who for half a day gave private lessons at the school to those who could afford it and then was employed by the school to teach public school students the other half of the day.

In the 1988–89 school year we committed $1.6 million for artistically talented and gifted children. That's in addition to the ongoing commitment we have to instruction in the arts, which was strengthened by the Education Finance Act of 1977. There is the ABC plan now that would provide a structured curriculum to lead young people through a series of learning experiences to make sure that the arts are part of the basic curriculum. As Harriet Keyserling has explained, there is a strong commitment to implementing that plan statewide and funding it at the state level.

We have also initiated a program that we call the Superintendent's Celebration of the Arts. It is part of an effort that I've undertaken as state Superintendent of Education to raise the sensitivity, awareness, and recognition of academic and artistic achievement. In our society, we have truly made athletics a religion, and we have handsomely rewarded the athlete. I read an observation that I share in discussions about academic achievement and artistic achievers. It says, "Whatever a society applauds is what it ultimately honors," and in truth we have not honored artistic development or academic development. In recent years, South Carolina has put a tremendous amount of effort into a program referred to indirectly as the Three A's—academics, arts, and athletics. I'm not naive enough to think that we're going to destroy or change this nation's love affair with physical prowess, but I am convinced that we can raise our sights at least in the direction of academic achievement and the development of the performing arts. The program referred to as the Superintendent's Celebration of the Arts is just that. It is our way of rewarding something that we honor in the arts. Through the process of competition and participation, we bring 40 state winners to Columbia for a day of celebration, recognition, and interchange. We recognize student artists in their particular field of endeavor.

There are many players in addition to the state Department of Education in efforts to maintain the renaissance that has been initiated: James B. Holderman, president of the University of South Carolina, and arts educators at all our universities and colleges; the Alliance for Arts Education; the Arts Commission; Harriet Keyserling in the legislature, who is unwavering in her commitment; leaders like Virginia Uldrick (Governor's School for the Arts)—all have created a momentum that is moving us in the direction we should have been moving in for the last 100 years.

Let me touch upon two model programs at the local school district level in South Carolina. Greenville County school district has provided a comprehensive and sequential curriculum in the area of visual arts and music. They have comprehensive programs for artistically gifted students in creative writing, dance, music, theatre, visual arts, and media arts program development and technical development, including photography, film, and video. The Fine Arts Center of the School District of Greenville County was established in 1974 to satisfy the educational needs of high-achieving and exceptionally talented high school students. It was the first magnet school in South Carolina designed for artistically talented students. It is a thrilling experience to go into that center and see young people working with performing artists and acquiring skills at a level we wouldn't have dreamed of for high-school-age students just a few years ago. The Greenville County school system serves as the physical manager of the Governor's School for the Arts, and that five-week summer program is worth visiting to see young talent not only from Greenville County but from across this state participating with professional creative artists in a relaxed learning atmosphere that is unmatched anywhere. It is one of respect and dignity for the individual as well as for the arts, and one in which children are talking about developing their skills and performing. How exciting to see children learning at that level and enjoying it, and teachers making it so natural and not something that's forced upon students.

Four special-interest schools are in the developmental stage at the elementary and middle school level, one in each of the four attendance areas of Greenville County, to extend instruction in the performing arts to elementary and middle schools. That program, in my judgment, is a model for the Southeast and for the nation. I urge everyone to learn about the performing arts education program in the Greenville County school system.

The other program to which I call your attention is in Spartanburg County School District Seven. They have a program that is, as is the one in Greenville, fully supported by the school board, and the community is generally supportive of the budget when finances are in question. Comprehensive and sequential curricula in the areas of visual arts and music are developed and implemented in grades K–12 utilizing art and music specialists, and advanced courses of study for talented students in art and music are provided. The board is committed to the employment of highly qualified arts educators. The staff are well qualified and properly certified and are active members of state and national arts education associations. Probably one of its most outstanding features is its string instruction program. Anyone interested in a comprehensive string instruction program for public-school-age children is urged to contact and visit the program in Spartanburg County School District Seven.

What I've tried to do very briefly is to touch upon three things. First, there is a renaissance in this state that is emerging faster than a lot of people are ready for. It has momentum behind it. Second, there are cooperative leadership activities (including those of arts consultants from the state Department of Education) that are making a difference. And finally, there are some model programs of high quality and high commitment that are available in this state for visitation and emulation.

The Theory Is Realized:
A Creative Arts Elementary School

Rose Maree Myers

The Ashley River Creative Arts Elementary School is a public school in Charleston, South Carolina. It provides children with the basic education offered in all Charleston County schools, but it adds art, music, dance, drama, gymnastics, and string instruction for K–5.

Students from throughout the school district may apply to attend this magnet school by placing their names on a waiting list. There is no designated attendance zone, and there is no entrance requirement. Students are accepted according to their placement on the waiting list, which is kept by order of application.

As an integral part of the basic public school instructional program, children enrolled at Ashley River are provided with varied opportunities for arts-oriented learning experiences. The infusion of the arts into the curriculum enhances and improves the quality and quantity of aesthetic education offered and expands the use of the arts for cognitive, psycho-motor, and affective learning experiences. The arts-oriented approach to the basic curriculum integrates all aspects of the learning process in the development of the whole child. Feelings, senses, and intuition, as well as the intellectual and physical self, are nurtured, with particular emphasis on critical thinking, individual creative expression, and social responsibility. The enriched arts curriculum has three missions:

1. *Provide infusion of arts in the curriculum.* Classroom teachers integrate the arts through an attitude and style of teaching that uses arts processes as naturally as books, chalkboards, and lectures. Infusion signifies that the arts will be incorporated through interdisciplinary studies. Using the interdisciplinary approach, teachers provide each student with learning experiences enriched through the arts.

2. *Provide pure arts experiences in each art discipline.* The child has the opportunity to experience and understand art, music, dance, and drama as creative forms of human expression. Through the variety of experiences offered, each child's talents are identified and nurtured.
3. *Provide interrelated arts experiences.* The school is committed to provide the students with experiences that explore the interrelationships of the pure art forms. The arts are an integral part of each child's education within the structure of a sound academic program.

SCHOOL-WIDE GOALS

The extensive interaction and cooperation among teachers of visual arts, music, dance, and drama, and teachers of the general subject areas, ensure implementation of the following goals:

1. To provide a strong academic program that integrates the various art forms
2. To encourage the development of aesthetic awareness
3. To involve each student in the enjoyment, understanding, creation, and evaluation of the arts
4. To foster self-actualization and the development of communicative skills through movement, sound, visual images, and language
5. To involve community volunteers in all aspects of the program
6. To serve as a model site for an arts-oriented curriculum

PRIMARY EDUCATIONAL FUNCTIONS
OF THE FOUR ART FORMS

In working toward school objectives, the following educational experiences are provided in the major art forms:

Visual Arts

Exploring ideas combined with the visual communication of those ideas through a variety of materials
Experiencing success and pride in achievement
Developing perceptual skills
Using verbal responses as a basis for language arts activities
Developing visual awareness and sensitivity to the environment
Seeing the influence of the visual arts on all aspects of life
Making aesthetic judgments and enjoying art

Dance

Understanding the elements of dance: space, time, force, and flow
Increasing self-awareness through the use of invention, improvisation, and exploration
Using the body as an instrument for nonverbal communication
Translating thought into movement

Drama

Organizing ideas within a dramatic process
Developing muscular coordination and physical and emotional control in improvisational situations
Developing purposeful, spontaneous action and speech
Interpreting and analyzing literature
Working individually and with others to present ideas within a dramatic framework

Music

Performing individually or in ensembles
Developing language skills through the use of poetry, chants, and word rhythms
Developing listening skills
Understanding the structure of music and its elements: melody, harmony, rhythm, and form

EDUCATIONAL PROGRAMS

The Ashley River School follows the general curriculum guidelines for all Charleston County elementary schools. There is instruction in reading, mathematics, language, science, and social studies. In addition to the basic curriculum, which is taught through the arts, there is specialized study in the following:

- *Art.* Eighty minutes weekly, offering an in-depth program in visual arts, including ceramics.
- *Music.* Eighty minutes weekly, offering choral, Orff percussion, music history, and symphony and string experiences.
- *Strings.* Eighty minutes weekly, offering violin, viola, and cello lessons to all interested students in grades 4 and 5.
- *Suzuki violin.* Eighty minutes weekly, for interested students in grades K–3 (parent participation required).

- *Ballet.* Eighty minutes weekly, for a selected number of students in grades 2–5, in conjunction with Robert Ivey Ballet.
- *Drama/creative writing.* Eighty minutes weekly, offering basic drama techniques (for example, stage direction, stage terms, use of voice, improvisation). Creative writing exercises are used to enhance understanding and use of grammar skills as well as to stimulate creative writing, which may lead to dramatizations.
- *Spanish.* Thirty minutes weekly, offered to kindergarten students; 40 minutes weekly, to first and second grades; and 80 minutes weekly, to third, fourth, and fifth grades, with emphasis on using the language (speaking), as well as games and the study of cultures of Spanish-speaking peoples.
- *Physical education.* Eighty minutes weekly, with emphasis on beginning gymnastics and dance.
- *Resource.* Providing individual instructional needs for those children who, because of a learning disability, are not working to their potential.
- *Remedial reading/math.* Providing individualized instruction for those children who have scored low in either or both reading and math.
- *Speech.* Offered to children who have any speech defect. Children are identified through teacher recommendations, with a screening process provided by the speech clinician.
- *Compensatory education.* A remedial program mandated by the state, providing reading and math instruction to meet the needs of those students scoring in the bottom 25 percent on CTBS and BSAP tests in either or both of these areas.

PHYSICAL FACILITIES

The physical facilities at the Ashley River School include the following special teaching areas to enhance curricular activities:

- *Learning Gallery.* A mini-museum that features varied topics (two per year) as determined by the faculty. Teachers "plug in" classroom instruction to featured topics of the Learning Gallery. Members of the community participate as speakers on related subjects and businesses. Artists visit to share related art forms. Field trips are used as an extended classroom when applicable, in relation to both the Learning Gallery and classroom curricula. Parent volunteers are involved in setting up the Gallery for new topics as well as in overseeing its use.
- *Computer Lab.* Features computers and printers used by all classes as an additional instructional approach (remediation/acceleration) or as incen-

tive/reward for various achievements that are determined by the classroom teacher. Parent volunteers assist in the lab when possible.

- *Kitchen Lab.* Features two stoves with ovens, a microwave, full refrigerator, sink, counter, table, and chairs; used by all grade levels for cooking experiences as part of the instructional process that helps children learn to follow directions and to understand volume, weights, and measurements. A parent volunteer works with children in the lab.
- *Science Lab.* Contains lab equipment appropriate for science experiments on all grade levels. A parent volunteer works in the lab preparing and setting up teacher-requested experiments for children.
- *Special Area Classrooms.* Equipped for art, music, Suzuki violin, and drama/creative writing offered by certified specialists in these fields.
- *Gymnasium.* Accommodates a physical education program centered around gymnastics and dance.
- *Instructional Television Station.* Each classroom has direct ITV hookup facilities. The Media Center (library) is equipped with taping facilities, allowing teachers maximum use of instructional television. Live broadcasts from a communication center to each classroom are part of the system. The Media Center houses VHS equipment.

Working with this curriculum for five years has convinced me that it is more important that the Ashley River School be a model for other elementary schools than a magnet school for our district. We have accepted students without regard for their artistic talents (intelligences) and found that they have thrived in this learning environment. The faculty and I believe that it will only be a matter of time before a similar approach is common throughout the United States.

Part III

CONTRAPUNTAL TECHNIQUES

The Artistic Intelligences Conference promoted cooperation among arts educators. Certainly each art form already had an existing network of professionals and advocates. During the conference, delegates met in parallel sessions to consider the impact of the theory on their own area and to work out the counterpoint so that all might band together to improve arts education. For each session a leader in the particular arts field served as both presenter and moderator, and a faculty member from the University of South Carolina served as recorder.

The chapters in this part of the book are based on the proceedings of the parallel sessions. Each chapter is in two sections: the opening paper by the presenter/moderator; and comments by the recorder, who is the associate editor for the chapter. At the end of each chapter the reference list includes sources for both sections.

7 EDUCATION

Artistic Intelligences and General Education

Elizabeth Vallance

The implications of the concept of artistic intelligences for general education are of interest to arts educators in all disciplines. In this chapter, I shall approach the topic of general education as "education, generally," including but not delimited by the more specific notion of general education, sometimes called "the basics," and entwined with conceptions of the liberal arts. The chief question is this: What are the implications of adopting a conception of intelligence that includes multiple and/or artistic intelligences, in terms of how we approach education in general?

I will start with a list of recent observations about education, stimulated by Howard Gardner (1983) and by other reminders of the extent to which traditional education is bound to traditional conceptions of intelligence. The following cases inform our thoughts about artistic intelligences in various ways:

• Over two years ago there was a national docents' symposium held at the Toledo Museum of Art, a biannual event that moves around to different cities. About three-quarters of the people present were from art museums, mostly docents but also some staff. The keynoters focused on art museums and what can be learned in them, and after a few hours I realized a vague sense of unease on my own part—I was actually almost embarrassed to remember that I had been a typical straight-A student through most of my K–12 schooling. I was embarrassed because it seemed to be the thing, at least for several keynoters, to acknowledge that they had been slow learners, or dyslexic, or otherwise not considered "able learners" by traditional standards of intelligence and ability. It was only after they had discovered the arts, and learning through the arts, that they had flowered as students (and clearly, in their capacity as keynote speakers, were recognized today as successful professionals). This seemed to be an instance of public acknowledgment of something we are today calling artistic intelligences and a recognition of the role that nontraditional education—specifically museums—can play in fostering human growth. I will add here that the importance of artistic intelligences is something I refer to every day in my job at an art museum—in conversations with trustees about the role of the education department, implicitly when I give a tour to fifth-graders, or when talking with classroom teachers about the uses of criticism in teaching language arts. Some parts of our collective educational enterprise do rely on artistic intelligences, but they are not mostly in the schools.

• I am a member of a task force of an area university looking at ways to improve math and science education in secondary schools so that students will finish high school, learn science and math well, go on to college to study science or math, and (presumably) do so at this university. I think I am the token humanist in the group, and as such I have deliberately not been especially vocal on this committee. But I have been interested that the members of the task force seem so unquestioningly comfortable with the "givens" (e.g., that math and science are appropriate academic areas for all inner-city students). They believe that math and science are top priorities, and the only problem is how to prepare junior high and high-school students in these areas. My colleagues are beyond questioning premises, and I cannot envision their attending a conference on "scientific intelligences." Perhaps I am wrong.

• It might be interesting to consider Dwayne Huebner's five "rationales" in the context of the multiple intelligences that Gardner outlines. Huebner (1966) argues that we value education in different ways, the first three more commonly than the last two:

1. The technological rationale is one through which we assess the effectiveness and efficiency of schooling. It fits nicely with Gardner's logical-mathematical intelligence and is perhaps best explored through that approach.

2. The scientific rationale pertains to how we learn about the processes of education. It is perhaps most often explored through logical-mathematical and linguistic intelligences, at least at present.

3. The political rationale pertains to the power relationships inherent in structural differences within the educational system: Some schools are politically more "important" or valuable to have attended, or to be promoted within, a concept best enlightened perhaps by interpersonal intelligence and its sensitivity to such relationships.

4. The aesthetic rationale refers to the degree of coherence, the wholeness, the shape, the beginning and conclusion, that is given to the curriculum or to the school day. It is a value we are unaccustomed to discussing; artistic intelligences might help us to grapple with it more readily.

5. The ethical rationale pertains to the collegial relationships among staff, the power relationships between adults and students, and the ethical commitments an institution implicitly makes when it brings people into contact with one another. The personal intelligences outlined by Gardner might operate to illuminate this approach to assessing schooling.

In any event, Huebner's five "rationales" are always an interesting framework and might fruitfully be studied through Gardner's more recent theory.

• Finally, a relatively unformed thought occurs to me: One way to identify the kinds of intelligences we are not especially strong in (if we wanted to develop profiles of individuals in this way) is to ask what areas are regularly mysterious to us, what areas induce a kind of intellectual panic when they are broached. In my case, electricity and computers are total mysteries, perhaps bespeaking either a failure of spatial intelligence because my frustration is in my inability to picture how they work, of a predominance of spatial abilities, in my persistence in wishing I could imagine them visually. Likewise, the "math anxiety" stage, which many young girls experience around the age of 12, reflects a reading of the relative strength of logical-mathematical intelligence in students by age and gender. I often overhear people in the galleries expressing exasperation at not being able to "understand" the modern art they are seeing, a tacit admission of an incomplete ability to work through spatial intelligences. And so on. We have many examples from everyday life of the "tacit intelligences" profiles of people as they process information through some intelligences and are frustrated by others.

These lines of thought might give us some fresh ways to explore how well we understand the artistic intelligences concept, and I offer them simply for that reason. But let us turn now to some specifically educational issues that might arise as we consider trying to apply the artistic intelligences concept to education in general.

First, if we acknowledge that many parents and teachers already know that some children are weak in the traditionally valued intelligences but stronger in artistically oriented ones ("He's not a reader, but he loves to make things"), then the larger problem may be the sociopolitical one of enhancing the status of the arts in society generally so that resources can be diverted to strengthening those talents more than they now are. The arts simply lack the status held by science and math, and they always have. The case for the arts is made even more difficult because what status they are accorded seems to skip over ordinary people and be assigned to the rich: They are seen as high-falutin' and a frill, something not really accessible to all. This attitude was reflected only too well in an advertisement I saw recently in the local newspaper, from an area bank advertising money market funds: "Now you don't have to be rich to make $50,000 look like a million," read the copy, and the illustration showed a turned-out couple at the theater holding a publication called *On Stage*. It spoke for itself, unfortunately.

Second, if we took the multiple intelligences concept to heart and sought to open education to all of Gardner's "frames of mind," what would be the impact on the structure of subject matter and how it is taught? Would we try to foster spatial intelligence through art, or through engineering? Would football and ballet be equally accessible to all students seeking to develop their bodily kinesthetic intelligence? Do all seven intelligences have so wide a range of potential subject-matter applicability? If so, how would we build a subject-matter curriculum around this concept? Or should we try to avoid the traditional subject-matter constraints altogether? I have no specific answers to these questions, but I do see them as critical issues for education.

Third, what if we could start over and redesign education to accommodate all the multiple intelligences equitably; what would we have students study, and where? Where would we start—with goals pertaining to each "intelligence" or could we start with shuffling the traditional subject matters and broadening their goals to refer to the intelligences? One way of asking how we would start over is by referring to Joseph Schwab's (1969) four "commonplaces" of the curriculum, four elements that it is impossible to ignore when talking about the curriculum: subject matter, students, teachers, and setting or milieu. We now talk about subject matter in the traditional mode of the disciplines, but conceivably we could reconfigure this element to refer more directly to ways of knowing than to what is known; conceivably too the setting of education could shift if some intelligences proved to be taught better in nonschool settings, such as in apprenticeships. We are unlikely to have the chance to redesign whole educational systems to accommodate the multiple intelligences first and other things second, at least not all at once; but how we would do so if given the chance is tantalizing to think about.

Fourth, I wonder about hierarchies in the way we assess knowledge. There is now a pretty evident hierarchy within the subject matters that we cover in school: science and math and language are "basics," or "solids" (a concept I borrow from a colleague who reminded me that in my own high school we talked about solids versus something else that was less valued), while the arts are often relegated to afternoons late in the week. Is there a hierarchy among the seven intelligences? Plainly, Gardner's work implies that there should be equity among them, but how would we avoid a rank order even if we set out specifically to do so? How would a hierarchy among the acceptable intelligences affect the curriculum? Would it result in a modernized form of tracking? Would it label students as irrevocably as current curricular tracks now do? We do not know yet, but it is a question perhaps we should be prepared to confront.

One especially interesting experiment in a redefinition of traditional disciplines and of their role in the school curriculum is in the work being advanced by the Getty Center for Education in the Arts (1985) on a concept called discipline-based art education (DBAE). Not actually originated by the Getty Center, DBAE is an approach to art education that has gradually been distilled from the available literature and coalesced into an innovative and coherent concept. The DBAE approach redefines art education "beyond creating"—that is, beyond the traditional hands-on, art-production view of "art" in school—to include also the disciplines of art history, art criticism, and aesthetics. The resulting four disciplines form the content on which the art curriculum would be based, with approximately equal emphasis given to each. Advocates of DBAE agree on several other characteristics of the art curriculum besides its basis in four disciplines: The art curriculum should be a written, sequential curriculum beginning in kindergarten and progressing through twelfth grade, and it should be district-wide. Thus the art curriculum would take its place among other established written and cumulative subject-matter curriculum outlines; it would, in our terms here, become a "solid," a "basic," a subject area with agreed-upon and diversified content.

The advantages to this approach to art education are many, but there has been considerable controversy about the concept as well, chiefly from art educators hesitant to cut into already limited production time. From our point of view here, the chief advantage lies in broadening the concept of art education to allow for many different kinds of intelligences to come into play. Traditional art instruction calls chiefly on spatial intelligence and traditional conceptions of artistic "creativity"; DBAE would also reward the linguistic intelligence involved in art-historical research, for example, thereby making the rewards of the visual arts accessible to students other than those who are "good at art." Indeed, I can easily argue that by including art history, criticism, and aesthetics in the art curriculum, DBAE may empower far more students to be lifelong learners in art than the more restricted traditional concept of art has ever been able to do. Discipline-based art education shows considerable promise for extending the subject matter of art to a broad range of students by calling on a greater variety of intelligences. For this reason, it merits serious consideration by educators interested in the concept of artistic intelligences and in its applicability to education in general.

All of this becomes especially interesting in light of current popular and academic interest in finding a curriculum for our common culture—Hirsch's *Cultural Literacy* (1987) and Bloom's *The Closing of the American Mind* (1987) being the stock examples, with the questions also raised in debates about "world cultures" and "Western civilization" courses at many colleges, including, very visibly, Stanford University. I tend to agree that a functioning nation needs to be educated in some shared cultural traditions that are generally acknowledged to be important. The question leads us to the concept of a more specifically defined "general education," the argument that a certain basic core of cultural information should be shared by all. The question always is, however, *what* core? *Whose* cultural traditions? How can we accommodate our pluralistic population?

The multiple intelligences concept involves new ways of phrasing these age-old questions of what knowledge is of most worth. If we approach the common-culture questions from the standpoint of the multiple intelligences, what are "the basics"? What do we most need to know? Without what ways of knowing would we be considered incomplete? If students can somehow "major" in some intelligences and not others, what would we want all students to have in common, in these terms? And if we could agree on all this, what are the implications for the forms that education would best take? We might want some traditional classroom lecture formats, but we might want more laboratories, more studios, more apprenticeship opportunities with master teachers, a greater variety of forms of learning open to all students—a scheduling nightmare, for sure. If we wanted all students to have some minimal access to all kinds of intelligences in the course of a dozen years of education, how would this commitment change the role of "electives," how would it change teacher training, how would it affect how guidance counselors are trained? And, as an end result, how would it affect how we all describe our own education and what we seek to continue in enrichment throughout our adult years—which, after all, constitute most of our lives? How might we redefine the aims of lifelong learning and continuing education in the different professions?

In short, our system of education has generally emphasized only a very few of the intelligences with which we approach problems in our lives. If we take the concept of multiple and artistic intelligences seriously, we need to be prepared to rethink how we educate all people, generally. Do we want to do this? And if so, where do we start?

Implications for General Education

CRAIG KRIDEL

Delegates attending the education parallel session needed little convincing of the importance of multiple intelligences. From the outset, the group recognized the misguided emphasis on verbal and logical-analytical skills in the school curriculum. The current proposals for school reform document this fact. We also saw how difficult and formidable the task would be to change this bias in our schools given the commonly held view that solid scholarship is, indeed, basically logical and linear. Throughout our discourse, however, we were convinced that we need not give up at what seemed to be an impasse. There are many opportunities for change—now more than ever if we can but recognize them. As a consequence, our questions became not whether it is possible to initiate curriculum reform but, instead, where does one begin?

Throughout the discussions, our focus was on the general curriculum rather than on a specific subject area or arts discipline. We addressed schooling at all levels—early childhood education through post-secondary education. Though our setting for educational reform was most broadly conceived, we were convinced that there was a crucial role for artistic intelligences. In effect, it might well be said that our group's contribution to this consideration rested on our examination of the overall, larger curriculum context for the fostering of artistic intelligences. Nothing short of a redefinition of the concept of general education is called for if one wishes to move beyond the impasse of a narrowly conceived curriculum based on an equally narrow concept of the nature of intelligence.

ARTS AND THE CURRICULUM

If only life and our lived experiences were as clear and direct as the traditional views of curriculum continue to be! The school curriculum is fragmented into separate subjects, standardized by accreditation agencies and post-secondary institutions, unified by pedagogical methodologies, and justified by a "sanitary" form of empirical evaluation. Simplistically, it designates good from bad, gifted from disabled, and above average from below average. The impact of this rigid evaluation system has shaped the public's attitude toward education. Testing, it seems, will always be endorsed since it embodies a commonsensical attitude toward efficiency and effectiveness. Yet, the burden of over-testing is beginning to be recognized by the public. Among the wails of lower test scores are the cries of excessive testing and the need for some type of change.

Multiple intelligences and the extension of the idea of artistic intelligences offer many programmatic possibilities for reconceiving the nature of general education. My discussion will focus on specific "roadblocks" for curricular reform. To do this, I will explore related ideas in professional education literature that provide sufficient support and guidance for such reform. My discussion rests upon one basic, fundamental belief: Artistic intelligences are within the realm of all students' capabilities. Too often arts education is reserved only for the aspiring painter, musician, or dancer. Or, aesthetic education is offered only to the gifted and talented. If students, especially at the secondary level, are not engaged in the actual performance or making of art, few opportunities for arts education exist even in large high schools that boast of their wide range of specialized offerings. A premise of Gardner's work is that the concept of multiple intelligences is applicable to the education of all students and should not be viewed as talents or learning styles for only a select few. Thus, artistic intelligences call for a reconceptualization of not only performance in the arts but also their appreciation. General education goals, in this way, require new formulations and different curricular designs for their implementation.

STRUCTURE OF THE CURRICULUM

We live within a separate-subject, discipline-oriented conception of education. (This conception is not as prevalent in elementary education; however, it does permeate all levels of education.) Possibilities for multiple intelligences force us to face a crossroads: Do we work within this system, or do we attempt a total restructuring of the curriculum? Perhaps the conception of artistic intelligences is embedded within the separate subjects and is waiting to be drawn out in appropriate new designs. Elizabeth Vallance's description of discipline-based art education suggests such opportunities. Could similar programs be developed for nurturing artistic intelligences within discipline-based music education, or discipline-based science or math education? Or, would artistic intelligences be best served within an integrated core curriculum where subjects could function naturally as broad problem areas that form the nucleus of the curriculum? Such decisions, of course, cannot be made hypothetically. The context for curriculum development is always a specific school-community setting. The separate-subject framework is so widespread that this may be one's only forum. As has been stated by others concerning standardized evaluation, tests will not go away so it behooves arts educators to take the initiative and develop more sophisticated standardized tests. Similarly, since we live within a world of separate subjects and Carnegie units, a pragmatic direction of reform is to develop the idea of artistic intelligences within this context.

Although an integrated approach to curriculum may not be commonplace in today's educational system, the idea is not without merit. Integration of school subjects in the context of a core curriculum has a long tradition in American education. We too often tend to ignore history in our school reform efforts. Progressive educators of the 1920s and 1930s developed the concept of core curriculum to its most refined form. Harold Alberty (1947) developed a widely used classification system of five types of core curricula in which traditional subjects were correlated and fused, to be replaced by broader organizations of knowledge based upon students' interests or societal needs. Such alternative conceptions of the school curriculum would raise questions today about the desired achievement of basic skills and cultural literacy. Yet, the Progressives "proved" beyond question that an integrated curriculum (incorporating the arts) provided an equal, if not better, preparation for college. This research project, the Progressive Education Association's Eight Year Study (1932–40), shattered the basic rationale for a separate-subject organization of the curriculum—the completion of specific school units as the best preparation for college. This is not to suggest that an integrated core curriculum is "better" than a separate-subject approach if the latter is conceived on a broad theoretical base, as Gardner's concept of multiple intelligences is. But it does reflect our need to explore alternatives such as the more functional general education core design that has historically proved to be very promising—especially for the general education of all students.

As entrenched as separate subjects may be, the possibility for alternative integrated curricular programs exists. In fact, the report of the Carnegie Council on Adolescent Development criticizes the middle school curriculum for being "unconnected and seemingly irrelevant" and suggests specifically the development of a core curriculum that integrates the traditionally separate subjects of English, the arts, history, and social studies around a single theme. And to provide further encouragement for those of us who are persuaded that there are, indeed, artistic intelligences, the report warns educators not to underestimate students' willingness to respond to creative experiences. This national report represents a valuable instrument for forging curriculum change in general education.

CURRICULUM DEVELOPMENT

Too often, curriculum development is viewed from a system-wide perspective. Curricular decisions are made by the central administration and then disseminated to schools throughout the district. Change is assumed to occur "all at once." Great skepticism and hesitancy result, since any suggested alteration raises numerous problems in specific schools within the system. This dominant perspective of curricular change coincides with most notions of centralized school administration and proves to be a deterrent to any type of curricular reform. As we discuss a reconceptualization of school curriculum to include artistic intelligences, an alternative to traditional curriculum development demands attention. The forgotten, yet significant, work of Hilda Taba (1962) provides this alternative. Taba's approach sought to develop and test the experimental programs in individual classrooms before mandating system-wide change. From this initial testing, educators may revise and consolidate curricula and then develop an overarching framework for system-wide implementation. At this last stage, the new programs are installed and disseminated.

By inverting the traditional approach to curriculum development, Taba offers today's educators a method to develop theory and practice without confronting the many top-down problems that serve to prevent change. Today's educators are beginning to support this inverted model for curriculum development. Robert Slavin's (1989) monumental critique of educational fads is but one example of this recognition of the need for a different model for curriculum change. He reports: "School districts that intend to adopt new programs on a broad scale should first conduct evaluations of those programs on a smaller scale, comparing experimental and control schools or classes on fair measures over extended time periods" (pp. 757–758).

By drawing upon Taba's work, educators have a detailed curriculum development process to assist their efforts to implement artistic intelligences programs into the schools and to generate more adequate general education curriculum designs for all students—not only the talented few.

POLITICS OF
SCHOOL CHANGE AND REFORM

All discussions of artistic intelligences ultimately revolve around the difficulties of initiating curricular change and of convincing educators that new opportunities for the arts must be addressed. Perhaps no time since the 1930s, however, offers a better opportunity for school experimentation and possibilities for the redesign of curriculum that would foster the development of artistic intelligences.

Recent statements from the American Federation of Teachers (AFT) and the National Education Association both offer this hope. Mary Hatwood Futrell has proposed that each state name at least one school district a "learning laboratory" where teachers could be free to experiment. Concurrently, Albert Shanker and AFT delegates suggested the formation of charter schools. Using Henry Hudson as a "metaphor" for school experimentation, Shanker (1988) writes:

> The charter had to go to a "grantee—someone with a vision or a plan." Henry Hudson, for example, had a vision and a plan, but in a school district the grantees would be teams of teachers with visions of how to construct and implement more relevant educational programs or how to revitalize programs that had endured the test of time. . . . The charter usually called for exploration into unknown territory and involved a degree of risk to the persons undertaking the exploration. There was no guarantee that Hudson would survive the journey or, even if he did, succeed in his mission. There's also no guarantee that a charter school will find better ways of educating students. (p. E–7)

A statement such as this offers possibilities and opportunities that should be pursued by groups interested in artistic intelligences. The outcomes and results of experimentation may be difficult to institutionalize, but a forum for experimentation could offer permanent standing for the integral role of the arts and multiple intelligences in the school curriculum. Futrell and Shanker are suggesting a seminal revising of experimentation and a restructuring of education. Details can be argued and refined in the ensuing dialogue; and, no doubt, any effort to initiate a charter school based upon artistic intelligences will be problematic, as is always the case with innovation. But, it was the spirit of experimentation that proved most important to the progressive schools of the 1920s and 1930s. We must accept today's problems and possibilities with that same spirit. Shanker (1988) concludes:

Over time, we can expect charter schools to stimulate a different and more effective school structure. But just as medical researchers trying to find a cure for a disease or product developers hoping for a new break-through in business don't know in advance whether what they're aim-ing for will be found in a few years or a few decades, neither will charter school teams. A demand for quick results will send the message that only quacks need apply for charters. It's also useful to remember that Henry Hudson didn't find what he set out to, but what he did discover was invaluable. (p. E–7)

If any basic idea can help to implement artistic intelligences, it is this endorsement of charter schools and the possibility of the emergence of alternative general education curricular designs. The idea blends with Ta-ba's method of curricular experimentation and permits educators to de-velop examples—case studies—of multiple intelligences/artistic intelli-gences schooling. Fortunately, a second step for broader implementation has been identified by Lauro F. Cavazos (1989), U.S. Secretary of Edu-cation. In *Restructuring American Education Through Choice* he restates the importance of alternatives in education and magnet schools as a primary method to reform America's schools. "In the current movement of reform, schools must be responsive to parents, students and teachers. To accom-plish this, schools need the freedom to change and innovate" (p. 3). Ca-vazos proceeds to announce several federal initiatives to provide momen-tum in the national effort on choice in education. Between the ideas of charter schools and "education through choice," educators have more en-dorsement than ever before to establish school programs based on concep-tions of curriculum design that honor the basic idea of artistic intelli-gences.

CONCLUSION

Perhaps we now have the forum for experimentation that is more suited to the arts than to other areas of the curriculum. The "on the fringe" status of the arts may provide opportunities not typically afforded to "cru-cial" areas of the curriculum. No one argues against the importance of the arts; difficulties emerge when educators attempt to discern how important they are in relation to the academic subjects. Perhaps now we may alter the role of the arts so that they do not "take a backseat" but instead move to the forefront of experimentation. And while not jeopardizing "the guarded academic subjects," we may display one exemplary program after another in our effort to build evidence for the importance of artistic intelligences in the education of all students.

Programs that nourish artistic intelligences will not become a curriculum "bandwagon" in America's schools. The idea is too complex and crucial to future generations of students. We do not want to develop a groundswell of early enthusiasm leading to eventual decline, as is characteristic of all of our recent educational fads. It is better to seek changes that are carefully conceived but slow to evolve. For if we slowly and carefully develop artistic intelligences programs—each different and each representing characteristics of our varied educational settings—we may be able to initiate examples of true educational reform leading to generational progress.

References

Alberty, H. (1947). *Reorganizing the high-school curriculum.* New York: Macmillan.

Bloom, A. (1987). *The closing of the American mind.* New York: Simon & Schuster.

Carnegie Council on Adolescent Development. (1989). *Turning points: Preparing Americans for the 21st century.* New York: Carnegie Corporation.

Cavazos, L. F. (1989, May). *Restructuring American education through choice.* Paper presented at the meeting of the Education Press Association, National Press Club, Washington, DC.

Gardner, H. (1983). *Frames of mind: The theory of multiple intelligences.* New York: Basic Books.

Getty Center for Education in the Arts. (1985). *Beyond creating: The place for art in America's schools.* Los Angeles: Getty Center.

Hirsch, E. D., Jr. (1987). *Cultural literacy: What every American needs to know.* Boston: Houghton Mifflin.

Huebner, D. (1966). Curricular language and classroom meanings. In J. B. Macdonald & R. R. Leeper (Eds.), *Language and meaning* (pp. 8–26). Washington, DC: Association for Supervision and Curriculum Development.

Schwab, J. J. (1969). The practical: A language for curriculum. *School Review, 78,* 1–23.

Shanker, A. (1988, July 10). Convention plots new course—A charter for change. *The New York Times,* p. E–7.

Slavin, R. (1989). PET and the pendulum: Faddism in education and how to stop it. *Phi Delta Kappan, 70* (10), 752–758.

Taba, H. (1962). *Curriculum development: Theory and practice.* New York: Harcourt, Brace & World.

8 VISUAL ARTS

Visual Arts Education and Multiple Intelligences: Before Implementation

LARRY KANTNER

First, let me note that the implementation of Gardner's work is primarily in the research stage. From the hundreds of presentations in the 1989 National Art Education Association convention program, I could find only one that directly related to his work. It was "Arts Propel: A Progress Review," presenters Gitomer, Sims-Gunzenhauser, Wolf, and Dobbs (1989). This is meant not as a negative statement but to put into perspective the newness of Gardner's ideas in regard to actual implementation in art education. Years ago, I was asked to give a presentation at an early childhood conference, and my topic concerned stereotypes and the art of a young child. At the end of the presentation, as the audience was leaving, one teacher rushed by me saying, "Not everyone believes what you believe." Needless to say, I was relieved. I was relieved to know that in the dynamic world of education, there are different and competing ideas.

In his reflections on the report to Congress by the National Endowment for the Arts, Wilson (1988) wrote:

> The constellation of arts education contains some very different planets: Music: the giant Saturn, seemingly self-satisfied, serene, and stable; Theatre/Drama: Mars-like in its promise of school life but now mainly secondary and extracurricular; Dance: little more than a satellite of physical education, more exercise than art; Creative Writing: Venus-like in brightness and attractive to the public but trapped in the hot gasses of language arts where the formula overpowers the poetic; and finally our own Visual Arts Education, Earthy, surrounded by a turbulent atmosphere, divided into disciplined new worlds and creative, expressive old ones, with its nations always forming and breaking alliances, waging

warfare, or spreading the rumors thereof. These planetary, practical, and political differences notwithstanding, this constellation called arts education does share a common place at the edge of our education galaxy. (p. 4)

This book brings together the representatives from these various planets. Gardner (1983) has, for the first time, provided through his writings a theory of multiple intelligences, which addresses seven different forms of knowing or "information processing." He does not differentiate a separate intelligence as artistic but considers that each of the seven forms can be directed toward artistic ends. This is accomplished (but is not a necessary outcome) through the use of symbols appropriate to a given form. The outcome may be either aesthetic or nonaesthetic, depending on how it is employed and in what context.

It is interesting to note the receptivity of many art educators, along with educators in other disciplines, to Gardner's theory of multiple intelligences. A question that comes to mind is "Why do we feel drawn to his particular theory?" Is it purely political, that we are in great hopes that it will at last provide the means for art education to take its place within the educational domain as an important and necessary discipline? Can we attach what we do to a particular bandwagon so we will no longer be requested to justify art education as a viable discipline? I do not fault anyone who would want to see art in the position of reading or math: Have you ever heard anyone say, "Why is reading or math important?"

Gardner presents to us possibilities of multiple intelligences, something not articulated in the same way, but long felt, by many art educators. A primary value of his theory, at least at this stage of development, is that it raises awareness in *other* educators and interested parties of the value of artistic production, perception, and reflection that will result in learning. Its value emerges within and across a multiplicity of intelligences and is more than "working with your hands," "seatwork," or "extracurricular activity."

PHILOSOPHICAL COMPARISONS

Historically, a number of art educators have conceived of development as having multiple dimensions. Most notable would be Lowenfeld. He viewed these growth areas as parallel developments (but not necessarily at equal rates) and having the potential for stimulating each other. Both Lowenfeld and Gardner express a strong interest in and need for involvement with the process. Both are concerned with readiness as it relates to motivation and learning. Certainly, my intention is not to imply that Gardner is a reincarnation of Lowenfeld, but once again to say that art educators can readily identify with Gardner because of their history of thinking of artistic activity as a basic human activity and the interactive multiple dimensions of such experiences.

Let us consider for a moment Lowenfeld and Brittain's (1987) areas of emotional, intellectual, physical, perceptional, social, and aesthetic growth, and the stages: scribbling, preschematic, schematic, and gang age. Lowenfeld saw the potential and interactive mode of the growth areas within and across his stages of development. The stages appear like undulating concentric circles divided by an interactive system of growth domains—like an individual fingerprint of each child, with no two prints exactly alike. In many ways, Lowenfeld provided us the beginnings of a way of thinking about the total child and his or her artistic development. We can approach Gardner's theory, without great surprise, as it clarifies, redefines, and extends our own understanding.

As Gardner (1983) has stated, "Surprisingly little work has been done by educational psychologists in charting the general principles that may govern progress through an intellectual domain" (pp. 388–389). Again, art educators have attempted basic research in children's art development. To mention a few, in addition to Lowenfeld, Kellogg's (1970) work with young children considers mental and aesthetic development from scribbling to early pictorialism. Kellogg considered scribbling as a natural and purposeful self-taught mark-making—the beginnings of aesthetic decision making on the child's terms. She viewed the scribbling as developmental, beginning with the basic scribbles, placement patterns, emergent diagrams, diagrams, combines, aggregates, mandalas, suns and radials, the humanoids, and early pictorialism. Whether one subscribes to her various stages in a way is unimportant; the value lies in her attempt to provide us with a means of considering early mark-making as a meaningful and necessary activity for the aesthetic and intellectual growth of the child. Kellogg also suggested that within the marks existed the beginnings of writing, with the shapes of the letters only a matter of learning where to start and stop. It is interesting to note that language arts professionals now view scribbling as part of the emergent language concept. This certainly fits with Gardner's theory of multiple intelligences.

The investigations of Golomb (1988) addressed the cognitive development of young children as observed in their three-dimensional creations. Golomb differs from Kellogg in a number of ways, most notably in questions of the universal qualities of Kellogg's sequence, and the effect of children's visual observations and intent on their work. Golomb was allied with Gardner when she commented, "To see oneself as a true maker in the

basic sense of creating a shape involves the mind, the heart, and the body
. . . the intimate contact with the material, . . . requiring more persistence
and a rethinking . . . leading to a deeper understanding of the object and
the self" (p. 38). Golomb here addressed in her own way Gardner's three
kinds of competencies, production, perception, and reflection. Golomb
commented that confronting these spatial concepts may have a significant
effect on the child's cognitive and artistic development.

An interesting collection of drawings of horses as a visual history of
the artistic intelligence of Heidi between the ages of 2 and 17 was presented by Fein (1976). She stated, *"Heidi's Horse* is intended to help observe a child's mind at work forming and ordering and savoring the results
of her decisions as she obeys the laws of visual thinking" (p. 8). Heidi
grew up on a ranch in California and rode horses at an early age. She loved
horses and learned to know their shapes, colors, sizes, responses, gear,
gait, and personalities. This proved to be a powerful motivation for Heidi.
Through her interaction with and observation of the horses, she selected
and organized and produced drawing after drawing from a simple, rigid,
box-like structure to complex, graceful creatures.

Hausman (1980) stated, "Learning about the arts, like learning about
language, is a function of individual need and inclination; it is also a function of social and cultural dynamics" (p. xiii). Eisner (1986) provides an
interesting parallel to Gardner. He contends that "the arts are cognitive
activities, guided by human intelligence, that make unique forms of meaning possible" (p. 57). In a presentation in Sweden on the theme "Art as a
Tool and Conveyor of Knowledge," Eisner (1988) described the role of
education and culture as helping individuals obtain those qualities that
exist in the world, in order to create their images. Thus, concept formation, the creation of images in one or more combinations of modalities, is
called forms of representation (such as language, visual arts, movement,
and mathematics) when given public status. The functions of representation (as described by Eisner) are to stabilize thinking into images within
a structure that encourages a dialogue with the process and materials, to
allow for editing, and to make images public by sharing with others. The
interest is often motivated by the uniqueness of perception and individual
interpretation. Eisner goes on to say, "When humans want to communicate, there are different forms of representation, some more appropriate
than others for any given image." Feldman (1988) suggested:

> I think a good eye is a form of intelligence that enables one to recognize
> similarities, differences, originals, copies, quotations, analogies, para-
> phrases, modifications, and inventions in visual form. The development
> of this kind of intelligence is the prime objective of the education of all

students. In art education especially, a good eye is surely one of the most desirable outcomes of studio instruction. (p. 22)

With this as only a small sample of past and present art educators who are interested in artistic intellectual development, it is not surprising that we are considering Gardner's multiple intelligences. He has provided us with a strong neurobiological and cultural base for understanding the complexities of human cognition.

THE TEACHER'S PERSPECTIVE

It then becomes each art educator's charge to reflect on these various theories in relationship to what we individually (or collectively, as circumstance demands) determine the fit of each. As new theories come into being, they are often given polarized responses, from "I won't consider it because it might or will require change" to "We must stop all that we are doing and believe in and change by adopting the current trend because it is the current trend." As is often the case with extremes, neither will be particularly helpful. In some cases, the trends are merely exchanging metaphors. My suggestion is to first look at what we are doing, what our goals are, what opportunities we want to provide our students, and by what structure we and our students can best achieve these goals. Certainly we should all be in the process of re-evaluation, in dialogue with the process, which includes ourselves, our peers, our students, and others. For some, this will result in a reconfirmation; for others, minor adjustments; and for some, major restructuring. However, as is proven again and again, teachers in the classroom will generally teach, or attempt to teach, what they believe in, within the constraints of time, space, materials, and their own skills as teachers. Generally speaking, if change is to come about in any effective and meaningful manner, then the change will emerge from within, often motivated by outside positive or at least compelling influences, and not by a Pauline experience.

What I am suggesting is that whether teachers are intrigued by Gardner, Eisner, or DBAE, they should look carefully at what is being proposed as it relates to what they are doing. What we are dealing with are educational myths, the embodiment of one's cultural values as expressed in customs, rituals, and celebrations. Those ideas, beliefs, structures, and objects that we appreciate, we adorn and pass on to future generations. It is the stuff that holds and binds a community together, providing the rules and boundaries. This is what an educational myth is about; accordingly the individual teacher must decide. Sounds logical enough, but, of course, there will be difficulties, such as the problems of contradictions, areas of emphasis, means, structures, and outcomes, and often terms and the shadings of meanings. What is happening in this country is the development of various eclectic methods. Teachers are generally presented with either a state or local guide based on some philosophical point of view. They attempt to work within it, or at times around the structure, and they will adapt it when at all possible to their own perceived needs and the needs of their students. As Wilson (1988) stated, "Art education in the United States cannot be characterized as one thing" (p. 4).

I want to describe a point of view, a look into my educational mythology, through an event that I, along with Marilyn Zurmuehlen and the sixth-graders at Two Mile Prairie School in Columbia, Missouri, experienced together. It progressed from an idea, through a process in context, to a finished product: We entitled the experience "A Journey of Clay and Some People" (Kantner & Zurmuehlen, 1974). It has now become a slide record of experiences with clay and with improvised firing techniques exemplifying the total art experience, using material from one's own environment. In discovering the essentials for changing clay into more permanent forms, individuals sense their continuity in an effort of enduring tradition and diverse manifestations.

As part of this experience, sixth-grade students dug clay at a local brick factory; we talked about the aesthetics of pottery fired in improvised kilns after looking at pieces of pottery and images from books; we reviewed basic kiln-building techniques before and during the creating process; forming and decorating were discussed; vitrification was explained; and the firing and safety procedures were reviewed.

The dry pieces the students had made were fired in two kinds of kilns they built: an open pit and a sawdust kiln. The children earlier had collected enough wood for the open pit to maintain a hot fire for about four hours. This method produced pots of varied coloration, depending on their placement in the pit. It required constant tending, and a schedule was worked out for all the children to take part in this activity during the school day. In fact, children from the other grades also participated through observation of the event.

Large sacks of sawdust for the second kiln were obtained from a local lumber yard. The children built the rectangular kiln from bricks temporarily stacked with spaces to allow air to reach the inside. The interiors of the pots and of the kiln were tightly packed with sawdust. Once lighted, this kiln smoldered for several hours and required no effort other than occasional checking. As the sawdust burned, the pots moved downward. In the morning, all of the fired pieces rested on the thin layer of ashes at the bottom of the kiln and, due to the reduction firing, were a soft black in color. The pots from the pit kiln were also uncovered at this time.

At the conclusion of the experience, we met with the children in small groups to discuss their reaction to the experience and to evaluate how art had mediated their experience of working individually and together, producing their pots from wet clay, shapes, and forms. This was a process in which they were able to be involved from start to finish and beyond.

The following excerpts are from the conversations that Marilyn and I had with the children regarding the experience (C: Child, M: Marilyn, L: Larry).

Digging the Clay

C: I was surprised that the kilns were so old and rickety. I thought it'd be a brand-new factory. I guess it didn't make that much difference.

C: I didn't think they had the clay factories by the pits themselves.

L: How do you think the clay feels compared to just mud? If you went out here on the school yard, is there a difference?

C: Yeah, the clay is a little more pliable. I think mud has to get wetter to be able to squish around like you can with clay.

M: You could tell while we were digging it, when you had clay and when you had something else in your hands.

C: Mmmhm. When we put the shovel down and jabbed it on you could tell when you hit the rocks until you hit the clay deposits.

C: I thought it would be deeper than what it is. But it was only a inch from the surface and that was all the clay there was.

The Sawdust Kiln

C: We had to lay out some bricks flat, first. Then we had to start piling them up with airspace. And then we put one layer of sawdust, posts, and then another four inches of sawdust; and then keep on going. And then we put a sheet of metal. And we put some paper in for fire. And then we started it.

M: And what happened to it?

C: It smoked all the way down.

C: You put a lid over it, a trash can lid.

M: Do you think we could use other things than a trash can lid, do you suppose?

C: A big piece of tin.

M: What happened to the sawdust?

C: It burned away.

C: And there wasn't hardly none of it in there.

The Pit Firing

C: Well, we dug the hole and then we gathered a bunch of sticks and we put bricks on either side. We made a bed with grass and twigs. Then we put some pottery on it and then we put some more, and then we made it a little bit thicker.

M: Why did we not want to start off with a great big roaring fire?

C: Because they'd all crack.

C: And then all those ashes and then the pots were down there.

C: That was neat.

Digging Up the Pots

C: We had to dig it out by hand.

C: Well, they done a little bit by shovel.

C: You never thought it would happen. You know you'd think the clay would burn up or turn to ash or something.

C: He reached in there and grabbed hold of a hot pot.

M: Without a glove on?

C: I said it would be hot.

Talking About the Pots

C: They were kind of pretty. Mine was half black and half red . . . that mushroom . . .

C: The ones that put the yellow stuff on it . . . that yellow stuff turned red.

M: Did you like ocher on them?

C: Mmhum, makes it pretty.

C: My mother is using it for a cream bowl, and my dad's using it for an ashtray.

C: I'm going to use mine as a bank.

L: What did you think about the pieces?

C: They turned out good.

Final Statement

L: What would you say if you were going to describe the experience that we had with the firing to someone else?

C: If you have a chance to do it, don't skip it.

C: I think I'd tell them that they really ought to . . . instead of buying their own, they ought to go out and dig it up themselves, because I got a lot out of that.

The experience is a concrete example of Hausman's (1980) three general characteristics of what an effective arts program should do:

1. Provide opportunities for personal identification and involvement with arts forms

2. Help in the development of understanding and/or control of artistic media
3. Present knowledge of a broader context of artistic efforts by others (past and present)

ASSESSMENT OF INTELLIGENCE

Certainly, another major contribution of Gardner's theory of multiple intelligences is in the area of assessment of intelligence. Post-Gardner, the concept of standardized short-answer, paper-and-pencil tests will not be adequate to measure the various forms of intelligence. It is reported that Gertrude Stein, as she lay on her deathbed, was asked, "What is the answer?" to which she responded, "What is the question?" Before we can establish a viable assessment program, we must know the questions. Burkhart and Neil (1968) suggested two types of questions—commitment and evaluation. *Commitment* questions are (1) What are you trying to do? (2) What are you trying to learn? and (3) How do you plan to go about this? *Evaluation* questions are (1) Did you succeed in doing what you were trying to do? (2) Did you succeed in learning what you were trying to learn? and (3) What procedures will you use next time to improve your work? Although the questions are generic, when asked they become rooted in the particular domain. Not only are they questions for the students, they are indeed questions for the teacher.

Feldman (1988) suggested that a teacher "must be able to see his or her subject through the eyes of the students; this calls for 'pedagogical empathy,' the ability to imagine that you are a student encountering the body of materials, tools, techniques, and ideas in the person of an enthusiast" (p. 21). I would add that the student should be actively involved in this process, not separate from it. Assessment can be accomplished through record keeping of various types: journals, feedback, product lists and procedures, and portfolios. The results of the assessment can be used to motivate, document, edit, refine, develop, and extend the experience. This is not necessarily a linear, but an interactive, model, and in most cases the elements are arranged more by the process than by a predetermined fixed schema. Of utmost importance is the interactive role of the teacher and the student. This is vividly presented in the research of Beittel (1973).

Another in-progress research project that focuses on the individual engaged with the process and product and using intensive interviewing techniques is ARTS PROPEL, which Gardner described in Chapter 2. That project is researching curriculum and assessment development in art by asking the following questions: (1) How do students learn? (2) What are the students' learning styles? (3) Can we prove they can learn? This is being done through the development of domain projects, portfolios, and intensive interviews. The set of exercises features productive, perceptual, and reflective elements (Wolf, 1987/1988), as explained in the following way by Gardner (1989): Production is the composing or performing of music; painting or drawing; and/or engaging in imaginative or creative writing. The element of perception is "thinking artistically," by effecting distinctions or discrimination within an art form. During reflection the individual steps back from his or her productions or perceptions, or those of other artists, and seeks to understand the goals, methods, difficulties, and effects achieved. The results of this research, using objective observation, tempered with sensitive, insightful intuition (and I would include Feldman's, 1988, "pedagogical empathy"), will certainly be of value to future art educators in curriculum and assessment development.

Implementation of the theory of multiple intelligences in visual arts education can address a major issue expressed by Eisner (1988) when he suggested:

> Once we recognize that knowledge is conveyed in a variety of forms, we have in effect made a wider view of cognition and a firmer base for school programs that develop skills in using those forms; and with a wider view of cognition, we are better able to develop a broader view of education, and we are better able to develop a wider conception of mental development and a more equitable array of opportunities for students, particularly those whose aptitudes are now neglected in the schools.

M. C. Richards (1988) told the story of visiting her sister, who had a son about four years old. When she saw him, she said, "Oh, Kurt, how big you have gotten!" and he said, "Oh, I'm much bigger than this!" (p. 24). Gardner's theory of multiple intelligences, replacing the old view of a single intelligence, provides us with this same potential: We are now much bigger than this!

Visual Arts: Multiple Ways of Knowing

CYNTHIA COLBERT

It is mildly surprising that Gardner's theory of multiple intelligences has caused barely a ripple in the field of visual arts education. As Larry Kantner noted, there was only one paper concerning that topic given at the 1989 meeting of the National Art Education Association, where hundreds of presentations were given on a wide range of topics. I find that somewhat unusual, given the often hotly debated issues and exchanges appearing in visual arts education literature that have resulted from Gardner's previous work at Harvard's Project Zero. However, visual arts educators interested in the translation of Project Zero theory into practice are likely to take note of Gardner's (1989) recent article in *Studies in Art Education,* which introduces ARTS PROPEL.

Perhaps visual arts educators have been quiet about Gardner's theory of multiple intelligences for other reasons. The field has been involved in an internal pedagogical housecleaning involving political and theoretical debate and conflict. The limited spaces in our journals have been at times consumed by this debate. The energies of persons who might otherwise have given a thoughtful response to Gardner's recent work may have been fueling the internal debate within visual arts education. Yet, one can argue that if opinions were strongly opposed to Gardner's multiple intelligences theory, manuscripts to that effect would have been forthcoming. The seeming receptivity of the visual arts education community to the theory of multiple intelligences could be based on two common experiences that unite visual arts educators. First, the recent history of visual arts education comes from a child-centered theory of education. As Kantner points out, Lowenfeld viewed children's development in the visual arts as a reflection of their emotional, intellectual, physical, perceptual, social, aesthetic, and creative development. Lowenfeld's influence on the current beliefs and practices in the visual arts is well documented; he and many other persons who have made major contributions influencing our field would not find themselves in conflict with Gardner. Second, many visual arts educators share a common elementary or secondary school experience. Many were the "class artists," known to teachers and peers as individuals who could draw, paint, or sculpt in ways that were thought to be superior to the ways of most children or young adults of the same age. The "class artists" are the children who do bulletin boards for the teachers, who draw pictures for friends to collect, or who head decoration committees for teacher-appreciation banquets and school dances. Because of these experiences, many "class artists" aspire to become art teachers and, after doing so, are perhaps aware of their unique ways of knowing. They would, therefore, have little argument with Gardner's work on that topic.

Kantner included an example of an elementary art experience (producing and firing clay pieces), with a few direct quotations from participating students, that subtly addressed the idea of multiple ways of knowing or of experiencing (Kantner & Zurmuehlen, 1974). His quotations from the Missouri sixth-graders showed just how many aspects of the process were of interest to the children. The comments were not prompted by teachers, nor were they attempts by students to seek attention or gain prestige within the group. An examination of the complete transcript of the students' questions and comments reveals their genuine interest in and concern for this experience, and touched on many different ways of knowing. Students commented on or asked questions requiring

- *Linguistic information* about terminology related to the processes and the origin of terms
- *Spatial information* concerning the volume of a clay piece and where it should be placed in the kiln
- *Bodily kinesthetic information* about the building of the kiln, the lifting of materials, and the digging of the clay used to make the pieces in the firing
- *Logical information* concerning the results of their actions, the return of the natural area to its original state, and the possible repercussions of these actions on nature

The *interpersonal exchanges* between students included sharing information and answering questions on procedures or effects obtained by using certain techniques, complimenting classmates on their work, and making observations about the landscape, the weather, and nature.

The use of an art experience such as a sawdust firing to illustrate multiple forms of knowledge was warmly received by art educators interested in artistic intelligences. I believe that Kantner's illustration was not intended to be viewed only as an example of a quality art experience but was meant to demonstrate to visual arts educators that in many experiences occurring in their own classrooms, a similar array of interests and knowledge are tapped. Kantner's example shows much about natural approaches to learning. Children's comments and questions tell of their involvement and interest in the experience. One might ask why we have veered from this approach or where do we go from here.

THE STRUCTURE OF THE CURRICULUM

Although there are not many educational examples of applications of Gardner's theory, teachers should not be discouraged from attempting to address more broadly based instruction in their own classrooms. Should we seriously attempt the implementation of Gardner's work, the curricular reforms needed would be vast. The changes that might occur in the lives of students who excel in areas such as spatial and bodily kinesthetic abilities and who would undoubtedly receive encouragement and recognition for their achievements in these areas (abilities that are now unrecognized) would make the schools more humane and tolerable for these students. Children who are considered failures or low achievers, because they do not specialize in the verbal and mathematical ways of knowing that our schools so often require, might have equal access to school achievement and the self-esteem achievement brings. In that regard, Gardner's work brings to mind the work of psychologists who study the development of what are believed to be feminine traits (such as interdependence, intimacy, nurturance, and contextual thought) against a backdrop of developmental theories based on the patterns of men's experiences, showing that the feminine traits are possibly undervalued in a society that has valued logical, mathematical thought to the exclusion of interpersonal behaviors (Bakan, 1966; Chodorow, 1978; Gilligan, 1979, 1982; McMillian, 1982). It is to Gardner's credit that he includes interpersonal, bodily kinesthetic, and spatial intelligences in his theory of multiple intelligences, as these are ways of knowing not often addressed or encouraged by our present educational practice.

EVALUATION OF
PROGRAMS AND INDIVIDUALS

The issue of evaluation raises heated debates among visual arts educators, in part because of their history of a child-centered approach to artistic development and because the visual arts have generally not been adequately assessed. Terms such as *assessment, measure, test,* and *evaluate* are controversial because there is not agreement among visual arts educators concerning what should be taught and when it should be taught. Any discussion of developing standard levels of knowledge for age groups or grade levels is frightening to art teachers. They fear that they may be forced to give up their academic freedom or give up the aspects of the visual arts that make them different from math or the sciences. Program directors and state art consultants, however, fear that if visual arts educators do not come up with their own measurable standards, standards will be imposed on them by those who know far less about the visual arts.

The use of a screening device to attempt to ascertain students' strengths in a variety of intelligences is problematical. The education community fears the misuse of such a test to place students on a particular track early in their education, or the prescriptive use of the results of such screening to balance children or to further strengthen their proclivities. Any attempt to screen intelligences would require a herculean effort and great care on the part of the education community.

An individual approach to the evaluation of student work and knowledge is strongly supported in the visual arts. Eisner (1966) has long advocated the portfolio review of all art students, where a student's individual progress can be charted in comparison with that student's past performance. Gardner (1989) also advocates a portfolio or "processsfolio" for evaluating student success. Teachers point out the realities of their own teaching conditions that make this kind of evaluation difficult (one teacher for 700–800 elementary art students), but they support the philosophy of evaluation that does not pit one student's artistic expression against another's for grading or assessment purposes. Visual arts educators generally support the idea of a "spot check" or "pulse taking," where a sample of portfolios of students of different ages from various geographic regions of the country is taken as a method of determining what our students know, when they know it, and what effect curriculum practices or school situations have on their visual arts education.

Visual arts teachers are in agreement in opposing the standard paper-and-pencil tests for the visual arts. Given the examples of how "teaching to the tests" is destroying meaningful content in other disciplines, testing is one example of what we do not wish to emulate if the visual arts are to be considered a discipline. Yet, some educators (primarily those working in administration and higher education) feel that it might be possible to construct paper-and-pencil tests that would enable us to measure, for example, what nine-year-olds know about the visual arts and compare the results with what we believe they should know. Visual arts teachers warn that any attempt to construct such measures must take into consideration the myriad influences, customs, and beliefs that make up the cultural values of any group; for example, it is difficult to accommodate in any paper-and-pencil test the differences in the experiences of children from urban and rural settings.

Another aspect of testing in the visual arts is the divisiveness surrounding development of the instruments and use of the scores. Teachers want to be included in the construction of questions or tasks to be used if tests are to be developed. Teachers fear that instruments will be constructed without their input and imposed on them without their consent, and the results interpreted by people who are unfamiliar with the goals of the teachers or the needs of the students. Because of common practice today, they fear that the test scores will be published in the local newspaper, comparing the effectiveness of their art programs with those of other schools in the community, county, state, or nation. Art teachers are distrustful when committees of administrators, professors from higher education, representatives from arts councils, and psychologists devise tasks to measure what they are accomplishing.

EDUCATIONAL REFORM

Educational reform is always possible, sometimes desirable, but often not far reaching. Efforts toward implementing Gardner's or anyone else's theories into school practices must begin at the grass roots. Lacking the support of parents, teachers, schools of teacher education, principals, and the communities in which the schools are based, many attempts at educational reform have created only a tiny ripple, when waves of change were intended. Historically, some of the most provocative, compelling, enriching, and sensible attempts at educational reform have failed because they were begun by well-meaning people in higher education and the implementation was attempted by professors and district personnel (superintendents, curriculum specialists, and principals). University laboratory schools were once ideal places for trying out new methods, but as their numbers dwindle, the task of implementing sweeping changes in educational practices and thought is increasingly difficult.

Teachers have a lot at stake when educational reforms are attempted. They must believe in the proposed changes and value the principles behind the proposed reform, or they will not seriously attempt to make changes. If meaningful changes are made, it will be because of the convictions of teachers that those changes are appropriate. It is easy to find historical examples of educational reform that failed because the movement did not adequately address the needs of teachers.

I agree with Kantner that visual arts educators should look carefully at proposed changes in educational thought and practice as they relate to our students, schools, and communities. Agreeing with a theoretical concern is easier than making changes in the ways we go about educating students. At present, Gardner is not asking for change. He is currently implementing his theories on a very small scale and measuring their impact. It is up to us to read his findings, observe his outcomes, and decide on their merit and their applicability to other populations. His theory adds support to our efforts to educate all students in the visual arts and to provide advanced classes for interested students; the burden of effective implementation lies with us.

References

Bakan, D. (1966). *The duality of human existence.* Boston: Beacon Press.

Beittel, K. (1973). *Alternatives for art education research: Inquiry into the making of art.* Dubuque, IA: W. C. Brown.

Burkhart, R., & Neil, H. (1968). *Identity and teacher learning.* Scranton: International Textbooks.

Chodorow, N. (1978). *The reproduction of mothering.* Berkeley: University of California Press.

Eisner, E. (1966). Evaluating children's art. In E. Eisner & D. Ecker (Eds.), *Readings in art education* (pp. 384–388). Waltham, MA: Ginn-Blaisdell.

Eisner, E. (1986). The role of the arts in cognition and curriculum. *Journal of Art & Design, 5* (1 & 2), 57–67.

Eisner, E. (1988, August). *Art as a tool and conveyor of knowledge.* Paper presented at the INSEA 9th European Regional Congress, Stockholm, Sweden.

Fein, S. (1976). *Heidi's horse.* Pleasant Hill, CA: Exelrod.

Feldman, E. (1988). Clay: Arguments for and with. *Proceedings of the symposium: The Case for Clay in Art Education* (pp. 18–23). Reprinted from *Studio Potter, 16,* (2).

Gardner, H. (1983). *Frames of mind: The theory of multiple intelligences.* New York: Basic Books.

Gardner, H. (1989). Zero-based arts education: An introduction to ARTS PROPEL. *Studies in Art Education, 30* (2), 71–83.

Gilligan, C. (1979). Woman's place in man's life cycle. *Harvard Educational Review, 49,* 431–446.

Gilligan, C. (1982). *In a different voice: Psychological theory and women's development.* Cambridge, MA: Harvard University Press.

Gitomer, D., Sims-Gunzenhauser, A., Wolf, D., & Dobbs, S. (1989, April). *Arts propel: A progress review.* Paper presented at the meeting of the National Art Education Association, Washington, DC.

Golomb, C. (1988). Early representational concepts of the human figure in a three-dimensional medium. *Proceedings of the symposium: The Case for Clay in Art Education* (pp. 35–38). Reprinted from *Studio Potter, 16,* (2).

Hausman, J. (Ed.) (1980). *Arts and the schools.* New York: McGraw-Hill.

Kantner, L., & Zurmuehlen, M. (1974, April). *A journey of clay and some people.* Paper presented at the meeting of the National Art Education Association, Chicago.

Kellogg, R. (1970). *Analyzing children's art.* Palo Alto: Mayfield.

Lowenfeld, V., & Brittain, W. (1987). *Creative and mental growth* (8th ed.). New York: Macmillan.

McMillian, C. (1982). *Women, reason and nature.* Princeton, NJ: Princeton University Press.

Richards, M. C. (1988). Education as initiation. *Proceedings of the symposium: The Case for Clay in Art Education* (pp. 24–26). Reprinted from *Studio Potter, 16,* (2).

Wilson, B. (1988). *Art education, civilization, and the twenty-first century: A researcher's reflections on the National Endowment for the Arts' report to Congress.* Reston: National Art Education Association.

Wolf, D. P. (1987/1988, December/January). Opening up assessment. *Educational Leadership,* pp. 24–29.

9 CREATIVE WRITING

Confronting the Future: Creativity and the Human Spirit

CAROL COLLINS

A few months ago as I was traveling to a junior high school to conduct a writing workshop, I took a side route through a quaint New England town. I was not enjoying this scenic detour because my mind was very uneasy about the students I was to face. For the first time in 15 years of integrating the arts into classroom workshop activities, it wasn't working. The students were not responding. They were belligerent, rude, unruly, and very disrespectful. The principal was mystified; I was mystified. My faith in humanity had deteriorated to such an extent that I was once again considering my stand-by fantasy of owning a hardware store. I began designing the housewares section of my store when a sudden apparition loomed across the road and broke my concentration. A massive 1920s abandoned factory stood ominously in the distance, covering two city blocks—a vestige of another era. As I drove near, I noticed I was about to go under a small walkway that connected the buildings on either side of the street. Bold lettering inscribed in the walkway heralded the words, "AMERICAN THREAD." "How ironic," I thought, "how sad. The American Thread has been abandoned."

I began to wonder what fantastic machinery, with winding gears and shining efficiency, once manufactured that essential product that was the essence of America. Then it hit me. This was what was missing in these students. This was a sign. (I often find great meaning in life through obscure by-the-road symbols.) These students, like so many of the students I've worked with in the past few years, had no feeling for a common thread. Their life is measured by conformity, peer pressure, mistrust, insecurity, and a basic repulsion to anything that might deceive them into having fun in school. They have no measure for self-worth, no sense of identity. I remembered the closing ceremonies of the Summer Olympics in Seoul. I'd found it highly significant that the planners who organized the march of masks for the participating countries could think of no mask for the United States. On the one hand, this is a positive proclamation of the rich diversity of the peoples of our nation. On the other, it is a horrifying indication that we *still* do not know how to deal with this diversity. This is the problem with our education. If we cannot discover and link ourselves by a common thread, a collective initiative, how are we to nurture the discovery in the individual? We have not learned to link or to integrate the diversity of learning in our classrooms.

What is the common thread? Is it our ability to achieve? No. The rising number of dropouts in our schools is testimony toward that response. Is it our motivation to succeed and persevere? Not really. Suicide among our teenagers has tripled since 1955. Is it respect for our common humanity? Obviously not. Drugs and guns in the school environment are paramount. If you had to define the one thing that connects us, that should be taught in our schools, what would it be? I think it is the one thing that is *not* given priority in our curriculum: the belief in our individual worth, the celebration and nurturing of the human spirit. With this belief, achievement, motivation, and respect become valuable allies. Eighty percent of the workshop requests we have received this year from teachers in Connecticut asked for two identical things:

1. Help me to promote self-esteem in my students
2. Help my students learn to work together

They have no sense of teamwork, no belief in themselves. We serve over 400 classrooms, more than 15,000 students each year, so 80 percent represents approximately 320 teachers, 12,000 students with the same problem—students who do not know how to work together and cannot enjoy their individual voices.

I truly began to question the reasons for this fractured sense of identity, of worth, and how it relates to the heavy decline of writing and language skills in both students and adults. What is it about our society and our education that denies our belief in ourselves and in our ability to produce? Human potential has been defined too much in terms of mere achievement. The worth and expression of each individual are largely ignored through competition, standardization, and testing. Although these elements are important in certain terms, they have overridden other human elements to learning that are crucial. Balance among the elements is the key—linking the academic with the expressive.

There are several common denominators among students who work with me in writing workshops. When I ask the question, "Do you like to write?" I am usually bombarded with cries of anguish. Only two students in the past two years have admitted they enjoy writing. When I asked a group of 10 college sophomores, "What is your favorite reading material?" there was a heavy silence. Finally, one admitted she read *Cosmopolitan*. Another read *TV Guide*. That was it. They didn't read. Common complaints among my writing students from kindergarten to high school are "I don't know where to start," "What do you want me to do?" and "Is this right?" Most students do not know where to start, are afraid to take risks and to experiment, are unsure of how to elaborate, do not know how to critique, and do not trust their ability to discover a voice within themselves. They really want to be given a specific structure with all the elaborate rules. They want you to give them "ABC," and they will dutifully give you back "ABC." Attempts at expression and individuality are constrained by what the teacher wants, what the teacher expects, what is right, and what is wrong. Why? I feel this is a direct consequence of our overly structured, overly academic, overly analytical curriculum. One of the most celebrated writing programs among the schools where I work has set aside the standard source books. Students simply write for 20 minutes each day. The teachers have seen that students enjoy the freedom of writing and look forward to it. Students learn the components of language by the simple process of application, by sharing their writing, and by critique. Another school uses a thematic planning process where science, social studies, art, math, and other curriculum areas are taught under one theme, such as "Chinese New Year" or "Colonial Life." Teachers have commented that the students have fun, look forward to each new thematic series, and build confidence in their work. These two approaches rely on *process* to get the message across. This is where the arts come in.

The arts *are* the common thread. Using the arts in any study plan is the *fastest* way I know to motivate, excite, and promote participation in the classroom. At the same time, the arts function on many levels or modes of learning, while extending expression, confidence, and belief in one's ability to create, produce, and work with people in different ways. The arts can define a curricular transformation that draws on the multiple intelligences of children and adults. The arts can define new academic alliances toward the development of individual selves. Let me give you an example of what I mean.

New Hartford is a small school system of three elementary schools. It is one of the few systems where, immediately upon entering a classroom, I sense some kind of overt joy in the students. Yes, their classrooms are not overly crowded, students enjoy a more rural home setting than near-by Hartford, and students know one another fairly well—elements that are all conducive to a more relaxed learning atmosphere. Yet a key factor to explaining the joy is found in one individual, their arts coordinator. I have seen the trust that the teachers, principals, and staff place in her innovative designs. What does she do that is so crucial to the needs of these students? I can answer that because of my direct experience with her. She learned of our program through Connecticut Public Television and called the station for more information. After she called me, we met for three hours, talking about art in education, its philosophy, and its potential, before we talked about her school or my program. This was a fascinating journey that few administrators find the time to enjoy. Her past experience with creative writing met with praise from teachers and especially from parents. We discussed how to employ new methods to extend the students' writing and verbal abilities. I found out that some of their teachers did a lot with writing but wanted new approaches; others did little with creative writing but were eager to do more; a few were unsure about using what we call an "artist" in the classroom but were willing to try. We established that the primary goal was to extend verbal and writing skills. Meeting student needs also entailed heightening motivation, increasing participation, and reducing inhibitions to express so that they would enjoy the process of writing.

Now it was time to consult with the teachers. Having different teaching styles and classroom needs, the teachers were given a "menu" of artists or creative writing specialists. The methods and styles of each artist were outlined in the menu. Each teacher chose which artist would best facilitate his or her individual classroom goals. This choosing is a very important step. Just as each student needs to feel he or she has a voice within the class, enabling the teacher to choose the artist with whom to work establishes the equality of the partnership in the classroom. Teachers then outlined specific goals, concerns, or problems for the class and discussed with the artist how to incorporate those goals into the workshops. This dialogue between teacher and artist is crucial. An artist should not be an independent external performer, with the teacher having no input in the creative direction. The involvement between teacher and artist is the primary factor in success, a point not realized by many art education agencies.

We then implemented creative approaches to the teachers' curriculum goals and classroom needs. Some of the workshop designs included journalism and interview techniques, and others used music, art, and creative drama to initiate poems and stories; for example,

• *Sound garden.* Five minutes of taped music were used to spark spontaneous visualization as students write to changing tempos, musical themes, and so forth.

- *Object dialogues.* "Found objects" were used to structure plot and se-quence in writing stories. A paintbrush, rock, candle, "slinky," drum, and shoelace become "elements" for characterization, setting, and se-quence of events.
- *Three-person poem.* Students were organized into groups of three. In a group, each student adds, in turn and in sequence, one word to the poem to form phrases, maintaining a consistent theme.
- *Statues.* A group of three or four students were told to freeze in an abstract position. On-lookers define characters and plot suggested by the "frozen picture"; that is, who, when, where, prior action, and fol-lowing action.
- *Storytelling.* Stories were read aloud to motivate students to read more and to learn to visualize sequences in preparation for telling stories in their own style.

What was the result? Students had a chance to *discover* that writing can be fun, can be collaborative, can begin with simple observations. Most im-portant, each child discovers a distinctive and creative voice within. Simply by applying creative techniques to the writing curriculum, the stu-dents' abilities can flourish. Teachers, especially, can view their students in new ways and see new possibilities for structuring the classroom environ-ment. Here are some of the evaluation comments we have received from teachers in New Hartford:

> "Students who were quiet became actively involved."
> "Some surprised me by how well they could give oral directions."
> "They are more willing to work with each other instead of against each other."
> "Ideas—ideas—ideas—on how to foster good group dynamics to replace the stale ones."
> "The children became more aware of their own power in writing."
> "They learned the possibilities of combining fact with fiction, of using and combining the senses with writing."
> "They learned about collaborating."
> "The motivating activities made the children want to write."
> "I incorporated the activities into my yearly curriculum."
> "As a teacher, I need stretching too."

It is often the "underachievers" who become leaders in these creative activities, who speak out for the first time, much to the surprise of the teacher. In fact, one teenager in another workshop at a correctional facility told us, "I gained leadership and self-control. I learned to trust some kids

I didn't usually hang out with before. There is a way to deal with problems in new ways."

The teachers in another town, Bloomfield, have helped us to analyze our activities. We planned workshops in all first- through sixth-grade classrooms, using puppetry, music, visual arts, creative writing, and drama to enhance curriculum designs. After the artist visited each classroom for a total of only three workshop hours, the impact was significant enough to be noticed by the assistant superintendent:

> This is one of the most exciting things ever to come into this school system. The curriculum was not only supported by this work, but extended. Through the use of the artists' media, there was true learning for both teachers and students. The movement toward an interdisciplinary approach to the academic curriculum began as a result of the artists from the Creative Arts program. A total extension came into focus when the artists came in and brought this interdisciplinary approach. Tying together all of the disciplines was truly meaningful and tremendously powerful. (Mary Smith, personal communication, May 1988)

What did the artists do? They simply used the arts to teach history, social studies, math, and science, with a participatory structure to make it exciting.

In the writing workshops, I have discovered one very meaningful problem. Students do not know how to add detail. I've thought a lot about this. I feel students do not have sufficient opportunities to appreciate language or to become sensitive to different levels of communication. Why? We have become a fast-paced, push-button society. Everything is image—packaged, processed for us. Students want to give you an instant, packaged product. They want it to be perfect from the beginning; they want to have instant success, because that is what society and commercialism sell them. The process of rewriting and editing is extremely painful to them.

My students cannot find the words to express their thoughts or visions. It is even truly difficult for them to *envision*. So, we've again turned to the arts to *play* with and to extend the senses through theatre games in order to help the students *see, describe, feel, react*. Pantomime is used to *show* students in a physical, participatory manner how to add information nonverbally to communicate a clear, detailed, specific idea. For example, a group is given a quick look at the word *blizzard*. Through improvisational movement and without words, the group must describe a blizzard. The rest of the class guesses the word by the movements they see. Merely "cold" or "snow" is not adequate. The students must add detail to their movements until the correct response is seen. By moving, seeing, and responding, students are learning to add detail.

The first component of any new design in teaching and learning must include this premise: The human force is a creative force. From birth, we are full of discovery, risking, reaching, communicating. As we come closer to adulthood, these innate forces become somewhat elusive. The teachers I know are complaining that each year, more and more and more is added to their curriculum, becoming a great burden. They have no time to play with or enjoy their students. Loss of play in childhood is beginning at a younger age, to our horror. In fact, one controversy in the Northeast is whether to hold back kindergarten students who have not "succeeded" in all curriculum goals. The element of play, even in our kindergarten students, is at risk. In a newspaper article, Eugene Provenzo, professor of education at the University of Miami, stated, "Play is the work of children. It is how they discover the world they live in and how they come to grips with the physical and social aspects of life" (Kunerth, 1987, p. D–1). We need to recapture the sense of play in our classrooms.

We have been enjoying the benefit of understanding that individuals process information in different ways, by different "modes of learning." We can start with Piaget's biological levels of learning and expand toward the more recent left/right brain synthesis of analytical/intuitive thinking. Bernice McCarthy (1988) adds more light to these different levels. She characterizes learners according to their main interest in (1) personal meaning, (2) the facts, (3) how a thing works and wanting to try it, or (4) self-discovery. She believes that "We must feel as well as think" (p. 15). We must use teaching methods that incorporate all modes of learning to nurture the individual human spirit and potential.

There is a precious, underlying joy in all of us, in every child. I sincerely believe that the arts are the link, the common thread to nurture and strengthen the human spirit. The arts are the link to strong, exciting, effective curriculum goals. The challenge is to use the arts for insight, guidance, and practical learning tools to enhance all levels of learning. These four comments from elementary students after participating in arts-integrated workshops say it all, simply and eloquently:

"It was a BLAST! It inspired me to write."
"I was the best I could be."
"I learned to use my heart."
"I 'usta' be the earth. Now I am the universe."

Implications for Creative Writing

Lyn Zalusky Mueller

These comments represent a coming together of many facets of educational life. The backdrop is composed of Gardner's past research, his recently proposed theory of multiple intelligences (1983), and the philosophical views of education presented by Taylor, Eisner, Greene, and others in this book. It is shaped by the current state of the research, theory, and instructional approaches in the field of writing. It is influenced by the connections that creative writing shares with the other arts—as illustrated by Collins earlier in this chapter. Finally, it responds to the hopes, dreams, practices, frustrations, and fears of teachers dealing on a day-to-day basis with students who are struggling as they learn to write. The intention here is to lay out internalized personal and professional experiences that provide a vantage point from which to view education and learning via the world of writing.

The distinction between creative writing and other kinds of writing appears to be problematic among those who teach "creative writing." However, the distinction, at least for writing teachers, may be unnecessary. For example, while in Chapter 2 Gardner writes mainly about poets in his discussion of linguistic intelligence, he is also guilty of being persuasive, expressive, and creative in his own writing. In light of all these observations, no attempt was made to distinguish the basic skills of writing from the creative aspects of writing. Perhaps further consideration is needed. Or perhaps the issue is trivial when compared with the larger educational issues confronting today's educators. But for those of us involved in the field of writing, it is both our hope and our dilemma that writing is considered a basic skill as well as a creative art.

PERSONAL PERSPECTIVE

I come to writing from being a struggling dancer. I come to dance composition from struggling with the process of composing. Perhaps this personal anecdote will best illustrate my progression.

A little over 15 years ago, I was sitting in a large, college dance studio pondering my midterm grades. Why, I asked myself, was I always getting B's in history and A's in dance composition? My choreography wasn't that great. Don't get me wrong—I had worked hard in my dance class, but I had also worked hard in my history class. Somehow, though, when it came to putting pencil to paper to show what I knew, something somewhere was getting lost in my representation. Something, I surmised, was wrong, not with what I knew, but with how I was representing it.

As I sat there, in what years later would be called my "metacognitive state," a startling thought occurred to me. I was having, I metaconsciously thought, an ah-ha experience (a term that I had learned the previous year in Psych 101). Could it be, I wondered, that dance composition and history midterms were really quite similar—that they both were ways of putting knowledge, research, and original ideas into some conventional structure? In one case, that structure was a dance or a piece of choreography; in the other case, it was an essay or a piece of writing. The implications of this idea caused my mind to race. So, composing is the key, I generalized. In dance, music, art, writing, science—even math—you can compose and communicate, only using different forms and different structures. Suddenly, I had the same respect for mathematicians and scientists that I had always had for artists. Suddenly, knowledge appeared to be housed in different symbolic codes, and crazy things like statistical formulas became worth learning about. The task facing me was the mastery of these various codes or symbol systems. And based on my limited experience as a choreographer, I knew that was no simple task.

Well, I never did become another Martha Graham, but my experience with dance composition gave some form and structure to my perspective on writing, education, and learning. That experience also gave me a personal perspective from which to interpret research about symbol systems, symbolic functioning, and Howard Gardner's theory of multiple intelligences. Gardner's theory, as well as the other works offered in this book, provide implications and support for research, theory, and instructional practices currently emerging in the field of writing. Specifically, I would like to address four implications of the theory of multiple intelligences as they relate to writing instruction.

THE WRITING PROCESS AND NATURAL LEARNING

The writing process as discussed by Murray (1968), Graves(1983), and others suggests that there are stages or processes that writers go through in producing a piece of writing. These processes can be grouped into the following components: pre-writing, drafting, redrafting/revising, producing additional drafts, editing/proofreading, and evaluating/publishing.

The common link between the theory of multiple intelligences and the writing process appears to be that both tap into or reflect some component of the ways in which human beings learn. In order to examine the ways we learn, it is helpful to take a look at a learning situation as it occurs in the real world, a child's world, outside the school setting. Let us take a look at what I consider to be a good example of a child learning to do something in a real-life situation—learning to ride a bicycle. What do children do when they are learning to ride a bicycle? And what do they not do when they are learning to ride? The first thing that they do is attempt and fail, and attempt and fail again. Successes are small, incremental, and few and far between. However, they continue to try, despite the pain that they encounter as a result of those attempts. In fact, I still have scars from the sharp pieces of gravel that were embedded in my knees during some of my attempts!

Obviously, what children do not do is practice discrete and isolated skills for a given amount of time as a prerequisite to their attempts at bike riding. In other words, they don't work on each aspect of bicycle riding in an isolated fashion. They jump on a bike and try it all at once, completely immersing themselves in the activity or the experience.

Integral to this learning process is the helpful, supportive role of a coach. The coach, although a competent bike rider, is very rarely an expert in the field. Usually the coach is a parent, an older brother or sister, or a friend. Always it is someone who is willing to play a supportive role without taking over the learning experience from the learner or assuming ownership. Certainly this coach must be someone the learner trusts.

Children will also actively seek out advice from other "experts"—other children who are master bike riders. They will ask these experts for advice—questioning them about the steps required to perform tricks, imitating their styles in an effort to develop their own, and getting assistance as they try to create and personalize their own ways of riding.

Some children will even study bicycling in a more formalized way. They may obtain books about bikes and bicycling from the library, seek out magazines, or watch other experts bicycling on television or on videos in an attempt to broaden their repertoire of knowledge.

Learning to ride a bicycle is a developmental process that takes time—time for maturity and growth. It does not happen quickly. It is a culmination of experiences that begin in late infancy. For example, when my son received a three-wheeler motorcycle from his grandmother on his first birthday, I was astonished at the intensity and determination that immediately characterized his initial riding attempts. Of course his first attempts were nothing more than a series of painful and somewhat unsuccessful events. But before the tears had dried on his face, he would climb right back on his motorcycle and continue to try and try again.

For his second birthday, my son received a larger motorcycle. And at two-and-a-half, he is working on mastering the fine arts of bicycling—braking, controlling speed, perfecting steering, pedaling, and building his overall endurance so that he can stay on his motorcycle all day long. He tries to take his motorcycle with him wherever he goes, and he stores his most precious possessions inside the well located underneath his seat. At the age of two, he is already a skillful rider with purpose and a strong desire to continue to learn and perfect his abilities.

The success stories of students involved in wonderful classrooms where teachers treat literacy acquisition as an extension of a natural process of learning are just beginning to surface. These students are like eager bicyclists—willing to take risks; reading more and on a variety of topics; talking to each other about their readings and writings; actively seeking advice, support, and praise from each other and from their teachers; talking with experts and published authors; keeping journals; sharing their experiences about literacy; creating, drafting, redrafting, and publishing; and actively seeking instruction that will help them grow as writers. All in the name of writing!

If Gardner's theory is a glimpse into that thing (or these things) that we call intelligence, if it provides us with a glance at what is referred to as natural learning, and if the success stories of students who are actively engaged in the acquisition of literacy are true, then we need to think of teaching more like the supportive role of coaching and less like the teacher–examiner–student–examinee model that has traditionally characterized teaching. Instruction should be structured so that a more integrated and natural way of learning can be fostered.

STRUCTURING SCHOOLS FOR LEARNING

In addition to the need for individual teachers and their classrooms to be supportive structures for literacy instruction in a natural learning context, the school-wide curriculum needs to allow for and foster the interrelationships that exist between and among the various academic subjects that schools attempt to teach. The success stories reported earlier by Collins point directly to the tremendous wealth of experiences that lie behind these naturally occurring interconnections.

Gardner's theory of multiple intelligences has frequently been misconstrued as a learning styles theory. What is being suggested in Gardner's work is not a learning styles approach. Rather, it is an extension of the previous discussion concerning literacy acquisition and natural learning. Schools need to be structured so that each individual discipline (including, of course, equal ground for each of the arts) can be offered in a way that is relevant to that discipline. At the same time, the school structure should encourage the discovery of the interrelationships that exist between and among the various disciplines. Gardner's theory helps us to see that connections and interrelationships between disciplines are real. He helps us to see that, as educators, we would be not only remiss but deceitful if we did not provide an educational structure supportive of this philosophy.

BUILDING ON STRENGTHS

Gardner suggests that it may be appropriate to identify areas in which students have strong proclivities and to use these areas as starting points for fostering growth. He also notes that there may be several areas in which an individual may exhibit strength. This facet of Gardner's theory supports the previous issues that have been discussed and also lends credence to this issue of building on strengths, a principle that is paid much lip service in education. Many educators attest to employing this notion, and yet the learning model that is most frequently used is one of identifying weaknesses and providing subsequent and targeted remediation. We have even gone so far as to identify weak students and yank them out of their regular classrooms to remediate them. Philosophically and educationally, this kind of approach makes no sense.

Elbow (1989) has pointed out that perhaps the best idea that B. F. Skinner and behaviorism have taught us is that of identifying appropriate behavior and rewarding it—shaping behavior through positive reinforcement. If we want our students to have a strong foundation of literacy events (Heath, 1981), then why would we want to focus on weaknesses? How can teachers build on weaknesses? How can a learner find success through weaknesses? Bissex (1989) argues that teachers can identify places where learners do some things correctly, and those are places, she claims, where teaching should begin.

Let me briefly describe two movements in the field of writing that are presently having great impact as examples of the power of building on strength: the whole language approach to instruction, and the staff development component of the National Writing Project (NWP). Based on current theories of oral language acquisition and development, the whole language (or language experience) approach to literacy instruction is an example of a teaching approach that capitalizes and builds on student strengths. This approach is anything but a deficient model of learning. It identifies what the learner can do, expands on those experiences, and invites the learner to participate in new experiences in the hopes of providing additional avenues of future discoveries and development of strengths.

It is a recursive and regenerative model, much like the model of the writing process itself.

The NWP model of staff development is another concrete example of this philosophy at work. Teachers who participate in a Writing Project institute work at uncovering and discovering the strengths that they have as both teachers and writers. They are provided opportunities for growth as teachers and as writers and are encouraged to expand upon these opportunities in professional arenas. A fundamental assumption of the NWP is that teachers are the best teachers of other teachers (Gray, 1988).

Another fundamental assumption is that university and school personnel must work in a supportive and collaborative fashion if real change in education, specifically in the teaching of writing, is to occur. This collaborative model provides for a community environment that places both researchers and teachers in a supportive environment for learning.

The successes of the NWP are many. Moffet (1984) has stated that "the National Writing Project [is] the best curricular movement I know of" (p. 1). Scriven (1980) said at the conclusion of a three-year evaluation of the NWP that the project "appears to be the best large-scale effort to improve composition instruction now in operation in this country, and certainly the best on which substantial data are available" (p. 1).

THE TESTING DILEMMA

As always, a major concern expressed by teachers of writing involves testing. Testing has become one of the "harsh realities" of education. Given the focus of the preceding discussion, it seems reasonable to include assessment and evaluation as a component of the proposed structures. At present, however, testing is an add-on to the educational process, not an assessment and feedback system. In writing, testing can easily become an integral part of the process of learning. Many, including Gardner, are experimenting with portfolio assessment, which appears to be a strategy with promising results worthy of further investigation. Just as feedback is embedded in the writing process, so can assessment and evaluation be embedded in the learning process.

SUMMARY

This chapter has presented ideas influenced by the other authors included in this book, but related specifically to instruction in the area of writing. They are ideas that require action. As educators in the field of writing, it is imperative that we address the complex issues of learning and the structures of our schools, and their curricula. Relevant as well is the perplexing issue of testing and assessment. This chapter has offered no real solutions but has attempted to present further illumination of the issues as they relate to writing. In regard to the attitude toward the field of writing held by creative writing teachers at the Artistic Intelligence Conference, they were all passionately committed to riding their own bicycles as well as to improving the ways in which they help others learn to ride theirs.

References

Bissex, G. (1989, June). Comments made during workshop presented at the Gulf Coast Conference on the Teaching of Writing, Point Clear, AL.

Elbow, P. (1989, June). *"This is awful, but I like it": The relationship of judging and liking*. Paper presented at the Gulf Coast Conference on the Teaching of Writing, Point Clear, AL.

Gardner, H. (1983). *Frames of mind: The theory of multiple intelligences*. New York: Basic Books.

Graves, D. H. (1983). *Writing: Teachers and children at work*. Portsmouth, NH: Heinemann Educational Books.

Gray, J. (1988). *Model and program design* (National Writing Project Report). Berkeley: University of California, School of Education.

Heath, S. (1981). Toward an ethnohistory of writing in American education. In M. F. Whiteman (Ed.), *Writing: The nature, development, and teaching of written communication: Vol. 1. Variation in writing: Functional and linguistic-cultural differences* (pp. 25–45). Hillsdale, NJ: Lawrence Erlbaum.

Kunerth, J. (1987, April 19). The foundation of adulthood. *The Day* (New London, CT), p. D–1.

McCarthy, B. (1988). THE 4MAT SYSTEM. Barrington, IL: EXCEL, Inc.

Moffet, J. (1984). In K. Oliver (Ed.), *Information and notes about the South Carolina Writing Project and National Writing Project*. Unpublished manuscript, SC Department of Education, Columbia.

Murray, D. M. (1968). *A writer teaches writing*. Boston: Houghton Mifflin.

Scriven, M. (1980). *Overview of the Bay Area Writing Project Evaluation: Evaluation of the Bay Area Writing Project* (Technical Report, Executive Summary). Berkeley: University of California, School of Education.

10 DANCE, MOVEMENT, ACTING

Intelligent Kinesthetic Expression

SEYMOUR KLEINMAN

How do you recognize intelligent movement? What is considered to be a kinesthetically intelligent act? These questions were prompted by the work of Howard Gardner, who has received a great deal of attention since the publication of his book *Frames of Mind: The Theory of Multiple Intelligences* (1983).

I have asked these questions of dancers, actors, mimes, athletes, and even some of my colleagues, that peculiar breed we identify as members of the "species academica." I have not been totally satisfied with any of the responses, and so I understand Gardner's disclaimer and caveat about attempting to address intelligence as a series of particulars. He admits that the categories he is using, such as linguistic intelligence and spatial intelligence, are fictions. He says, "Nature brooks no sharp discontinuities" (p. 70). His intent is to "illuminate scientific issues" and to devise "scientific constructs" (p. 70). But, in the end, even he has to resort to resting his case in the realm of the intuitive. Gardner quotes the poet Karl Shapiro (and wisely so): "Genius in poetry is probably only the intuitive knowledge of form. . . . Nothing can tell the poet which words to use . . . except his own intuitive knowledge of form" (p. 83).

I like that. I like the phrase, "intuitive knowledge of form." I like it intuitively. It reminds me of the phrase "artful knowing" coined by one of my graduate students (Gim, 1989). I will come back to this intriguing notion of artful knowing, but first I wish to address, and also to question, an approach to intelligence in the arts through scientific constructs, "useful fictions." Are they really useful in the arts, in the realm of expression, and particularly in the realm of kinesthetic expression? My questions not withstanding, I do want to state my admiration for Howard Gardner's contributions. He has raised some very serious issues and demonstrates

123

clearly the shortcomings of, and danger in, continuing to treat the concept of intelligence in traditional ways.

ART AS A GLOBAL EXPERIENCE

I have no quarrel with scientific constructs and useful fictions as hypothetical models in the sciences or even as a literary form in the arts. They are effective devices. However, I am obligated to express, at the outset, my conviction about the nature of science and art, which establishes the grounds of my argument. It's a conviction based on some hypotheses about these realms or categories of human expression and experience.

My conception of art (or the arts) is global; that is, I see art as a dimension of experience that encompasses and transcends categories such as science. What I mean is that I believe one can do science artistically, but I do not think it possible to do art scientifically. In fact, I will go so far as to say that doing science is essentially an artistic enterprise. Or, in other words, good science is good art, poor science is bad art. This point of view leads me to offer another way of identifying the factors that generate art, factors that result in the creation and use of art forms providing access to artful knowing.

Any attempt to transcend the ordinary challenges us to use forms in ways that are extraordinary. If language is the form we choose, or are restricted to, then words must become "literary," formulae and symbols must achieve an elegance. It matters not if the enterprise is science or art. The goal is the same, a higher and deeper level of truth. In a sense, we academics create our own problems by our addiction to categories and reliance on words to provide understanding. But if we are going to depend on them so exclusively, we had better prepare them well and use them in a way that results in producing literature, artful knowing.

Artists continually deal with important questions and themes, and must cope with and stretch the limits of the forms and categories academics and critics place them into. Good art, intelligent art, results when artists find ingenious ways to resolve problems and defy these categories.

An example that is particularly appropriate is the work of Umberto Boccioni (1882–1916). Boccioni insisted that an artist could portray continuous movement and synthesize it in a single image. He expressed it in the form of an equation:

ABSOLUTE MOTION + RELATIVE MOTION = DYNAMISM.
This dynamism avoided . . . bogus methods of rendering movement. . . . Boccioni believed that the artist must find a single form of

continuous movement that would suggest the immediate past and future of the action and the interpenetration of object and environment that is generated by it. (Kern, 1983, pp. 120, 122)

In 1913, Boccioni created "Unique Forms of Continuity in Space." Kern (1983) regards the work to be a masterpiece, describing it as follows:

> The head is a montage of skull, helmet, and machine parts with a sword hilt for a face. The forward thrust of the figure is balanced by calves that are shaped like exhaust flames, suggesting propulsive energy and speed of movement. Its thigh muscles are contoured for strength and aerodynamic efficiency. The torso is armless, but the shoulders, fanned out like budding wings, suggest another source of continuous movement. (p. 122)

However, Boccioni's success in achieving a synthesis of continuous movement in a single image may be measured by the immediate somatic response to the work, an experience of artful knowing. I agree with Kern's description of the work as a masterpiece, but more on the basis of my kinesthetic involvement in it than on the words he uses to describe it.

At any rate, what I am suggesting is that it takes artistic intelligence to resolve problems well. In fact, I would go so far as to say that any expression of intelligence is essentially artistic. But what does this mean? Is it a discriminate set of behaviors, inclinations that are isolatable, identifiable? I think not. I believe that expressions of intelligence are revealed in infinite ways through a variety of "forms." The forms provide avenues or pathways of expression. They challenge our capacities to articulate and demonstrate understanding. For example, every art form relies on the active use of past and present sense experience to impart meaning and to communicate ideas. However, it is difficult, if not impossible, to conceive of having an experience that can be identified as consisting exclusively of only one of the senses; that is, an experience that is totally auditory or entirely visual or kinesthetic or tactile.

The good Bishop Berkeley was quite right in declaring that it makes no sense to speak of reality, or consciousness, or identity outside the realm of the senses. Our sense perceptions provide us with the experience and concept of *place* that, in reality, *is* our consciousness. The nature of consciousness is our *sense of place*. What I am really saying is that it is impossible to use or experience sense in isolation, in a vacuum, because an experience immediately imparts and establishes a sense of place incorporating, at the very least, an awareness of space and time. So, at the outset, experience exhibits a complexity that is at the very roots of consciousness. Space and time themselves confront us with multidimensional sensory experience. Therefore, no art form, real or imagined, actual or potential, can be conceived to be anything less than multidimensional. We know that visual art is dependent not only on seeing, or the sense of sight. And music is not based solely on the auditory. Although we place the arts into categories (kinesthetic, linguistic, spatial, and so forth), it's obvious that no art can be produced or experienced without calling into play and relying on a host of sensual qualities in a dizzying array and combination of impressions and feelings. This is a "given" of the human condition. And, in turn, it results in our sense of place, our identity, our consciousness being displayed as the ability to distinguish between subject and object, self and other. It is this distinction that makes art possible. Art thus becomes inextricably entwined with the world of possibilities, and the forms it may take are infinite. In fact, it is this realization of possibilities that really distinguishes art from science. Traditional science has restricted itself to, and deals with, a world of probabilities, whereas art, of necessity, must see the world as one of possibilities.

Some of these art forms, at first glance, appear to be more reliant on, and appeal to, one sense more than others. The "visual arts," for example, seem to rely, to a great extent, on seeing. However, while sight may be necessary to experience a painting, it surely is not sufficient to express it totally. The artist certainly uses more than his or her eyes to bring the work into being. And the viewer has no choice but do likewise upon encountering the work. In fact, it is entirely possible, if not probable, that the other senses, no matter how we identify them—tactile, kinesthetic, olfactory—may be even more crucial to the creation and the experiencing of the work. What I am suggesting is that categorizing the arts themselves is essentially nothing more than useful fictions developed by critics, consumers, and academicians, scientific and otherwise.

If we attend to what artists themselves *do,* we can see that contrived categories and constructs mean little to them. Dancer-choreographer Trisha Brown is a prime example. She has explored movement in relation to architecture, and in a new work she collaborates with Robert Rauschenberg, who produced a series of towers containing lighting and sound equipment and sensors triggered by the dancers' movements. Music, dance, and the visual arts synthesize so completely in the work that even the newly invented category of "performance art" seems inappropriate.

The development of these fictions and constructs may be useful and may satisfy our penchant for order but only insofar as they provide a stimulus to get the conversation going. The following comments from some young painters and sculptors are illustrative:

"I wanted a person's whole body to react to the work." (Barbara Gray-bill)

My work "gives me license to explore color, harmony, movement, and order." (Jay Ledner)

Artist Bao-Ling Hsiao, who has also studied music, depicts people walking. "It's a fascinating gesture and one which defines the city's energy." (World of the Studio, 1989, pp. 12–13)

All these statements affirm that artistic expression, no matter what form it takes ostensibly, deals with so many aspects of sensory experience that one cannot identify where one form leaves off and another begins.

The construction and identification of form appeal to the rational in us and our seeming inclination to seek closure and completeness. But the world of "possibilities" cannot tolerate, for long, a world of completeness. So, artists, and by that I mean anyone who sees the world in artistic terms, challenge and sometimes threaten those who don't face it that way. Often the challenge becomes a confrontation. Witness the recent events at the Chicago Art Institute, where the American flag was placed on the floor, daring people to step on it.

CENTRAL ROLE
OF THE KINESTHETIC IN ART

Now, I wish to address specifically the role of the kinesthetic and its relation to all of this because I believe the kinesthetic to be at the heart of artistic intelligence.

The kinesthetic establishes the bodily presence of place. This kinesthetic sense must be present if we are to have a lived sense of space and time or to have any awareness at all of sense perception. Every experience is kinesthetic, and my expression of an idea and your comprehension of it are kinesthetic acts. In order to understand this, I am suggesting that we develop and implement a kinesthetic or somatic phenomenology, a description of lived experience that provides us with the data and evidence of kinesthetic intelligence.

I will offer a few examples of what I consider to be expressions of artistic intelligence based on memorable personal experiences. First and foremost, I regard them to be kinesthetic because they provoked an immediate bodily response and appreciation resulting in "artful knowing."

More years ago than I care to count, I was involved in a production of *West Side Story*. I was a Jet. One of the climactic scenes is "The Rumble," which involves a knife fight between Bernardo and Tony while the gang members look on. At this particular performance, Tony, who is supposed to stab Bernardo, lost his knife during the course of the fighting. The entire cast was struck dumb by this turn of events. We were shocked and at a loss to see how Tony would deal with this unexpected happening. There we were in front of 3,000 people, not knowing what to do or how we could help. Tony, in a remarkable display of kinesthetic intelligence, grabbed Bernardo's arm and, turning the knife on him, stabbed Bernardo with his own knife. Our collective relief and exhilaration resulted in a spirited and energetic conclusion to the scene. I have always considered "Tony's" act as an awesome demonstration of intelligent behavior.

A few years later, I experienced another fascinating event. It concerned a young woman who was a member of our University Dance Company. She was regarded as a competent dancer but certainly not one who displayed much promise of becoming a soloist or being cast in a principal role. During rehearsals, she blended in very nicely with the rest of the corps and was accepted as a good, solid performer. In her senior year at one of the company's major concerts, I saw this woman emerge from being merely a member of a group to become one of that group who had a *presence,* one who commanded the viewers' attention. Something happened to her and to the audience during the performance I am describing that caused us literally to rivet upon her as she moved on stage. This was something we, in the company, were shocked into seeing. From that time on, we saw and felt her in an entirely new way. This, too, I have always regarded as a memorable display of kinesthetic intelligence.

Let me offer just one more illustration: A seven-year-old boy, after approximately six months of piano lessons, is working diligently with his teacher. The teacher is moving with him slowly through a short classical piece of music. He then asks the youngster to play it with both hands, up to tempo. The boy begins and gradually increases the tempo as the teacher offers verbal cues, and as they are responding to one another, the dynamics, the rhythm, the expression come together, and the scene is transformed into a powerful performance of the work. When it's finished, the teacher looks shaken and turns to the parent, who has been observing all this, and, with an expression of admiration and awe, says to the parent, "I must see him more often. There's nothing he can't do." This, too, I have always regarded as a remarkable piece of evidence of kinesthetic intelligence.

A kinesthetic or somatic phenomenology also reveals to us the limits of language in coming to grips with artistic intelligence. Scientific and even symbolic constructs give way to existential insight. Probably the closest language takes us to revelation is in the form of poetry. In poetry, words achieve a higher level of literacy and enter the realm of the arts.

Since, in this place words are all that I have at my command, I offer a poem in an attempt to impart my meaning:

Word and action merge,
Becoming deed.
Speech and gesture become one;
The word and the flesh are one:
Mouth and hand,
Torso and head,
Heart and mind,
Breath and soul.
All organs of expression,
Orgasmic, organic pathways,
Wholeness in practice and performance,
All into one;
All are one.

The intelligent act in the experiential world is a holistic act that, in turn, when experienced holistically, results in unifying the artist, the work, and the perceiver. In the final analysis, it may be summed up by saying that artistic intelligence is expressed and displayed in a variety of ways and through a variety of forms. The ways are infinite, and the forms are flexible.

Implications for Movement

Peter Werner

In *Frames of Mind,* Gardner (1983) established the concept that there are multiple intelligences rather than one general intelligence. This deviation from past psychological theory provides a useful framework and explains why individuals may exhibit talent in one area and be quite normal or even below average in other areas. Within the area of bodily kinesthetic intelligence, we must remember that there are further defined components of body awareness, space awareness, effort actions, and relationships (BSER).

These factors also interact continuously with other forms of intelligence (spatial, musical, linguistic, and so on) to provide a more complete profile of individuals as they progress through school. To quote Kleinman, "in the final analysis, . . . artistic intelligence is expressed and displayed in a variety of ways and through a variety of forms. The ways are infinite, and the forms are flexible."

As one would expect, the delegates attending the Artistic Intelligences Conference were already proponents of the theory of multiple intelligences, and were interested in the possibility of including the arts as basic to reform in education. We were all believers, dreamers. While recognizing that most curricular approaches to schooling currently emphasize verbal and logical-analytical skills, we came together to discuss the role the arts might play in education in a democracy. More specifically, delegates in the dance, movement, and acting group each came with a background and vested interest in improving her or his art form in the schools. We came to say "yes" to the theory of multiple intelligences. We came to question the possibilities of testing in the arts. We came to learn about model programs in the arts and what others were doing. We came to be a support group in fostering the role of the arts as the reform process continues in education. What follows is a summary of the topics of discussion and expressed concerns of the dance/movement/acting group.

FRAGMENTATION
VERSUS HOLISTIC EDUCATION

Public schools currently offer a separate-subject-discipline approach to education. Concern was expressed with this fragmented approach to school curriculum. In a so-called "egg carton" curriculum, the subjects of math, language arts, science, social studies, art, music, and dance are taught separately. Relationships between and among subjects are never brought into perspective. Those in attendance at the conference reflected a preference for a more holistic approach to an integrative arts curriculum.

At the same time, there was concern about the arts being integrated into school curricula in a way that they would lose their identity. Dance as a discipline has its own body of knowledge, and while concepts from science, language arts, math, or music, for example, may be interwoven, emphasis must be placed on creative movement expression. An integrative model cannot be contrived. Each subject matter must keep its form without sacrifice so as not to dilute the art forms through integration.

As Gardner pointed out, there are many ways of knowing. Artistic intelligence cannot be fragmented. Musical intelligence is inclusive of kinesthetic, spatial, visual, and verbal intelligences. We should not destroy a sense of intelligence by fragmenting art forms. After all, there is only a fine line between kinesthetic intelligence being used by a surgeon or mechanic (science) and a sculptor or dancer (artist).

ARTS VERSUS ACADEMICS

Over time, the public has developed an attitude/opinion/impression that there is a separation between arts and academics. The public views them as different and values them differently. The fact is that each of the arts has its own academic base/discipline. After Margaret H'Doubler (1966) established the dance program at the University of Wisconsin, universities began offering credit and degree programs to study dance. At the university level, dance programs continue to award credits and degrees, and courses are evaluated and graded on the same basis as other subjects. In the public schools (K–12), however, dance and the other arts often carry fewer credits than courses in the academic disciplines and are often graded on a different scale (for effort, attendance) or on a pass/fail basis. All teachers in the arts must work very hard in the future to change the public's opinion of the arts and their place in the academic curriculum. The arts are basic to education, and they are discipline-based in their own right.

THE ARTS FOR WHOM?

To establish literacy, education in the arts must be for everyone. General education must go beyond reading, writing, and computing. And experiences in the arts must go beyond doing to include historical and aesthetical readings and discussion. General knowledge in the arts can then become as basic as the three R's.

Through experiences in the arts for all, those with special talents (dance, movement, acting) will emerge. As it becomes evident that individuals are gifted and motivated to develop their talents, special opportunities must be created to optimize these talents. Attendance at magnet schools created for emphasis on education in the arts, special master lessons with professionals in the local schools, or advanced placement in college or university coursework are possibilities that might be used to satisfy the needs of the gifted and talented.

TIME ALLOTMENT FOR THE ARTS

Time allotments for the arts are often determined by state-defined minimal programs (DMP). After time is allotted to each of the disciplinary subject areas, there is only approximately 5 percent of the time left for the arts. This is clearly not enough time, especially with the potential impact that testing has in the arts. As the arts are process-oriented, students need time to explore, create, and perform. There are two ways in which this can be accomplished: One is to continue to lobby with school boards and legislatures for more allotted time. The second is to work with classroom teachers as allies so they too will create time for the arts. In this way, classroom teachers can use a thematic approach to an integrative arts curriculum, and specialists in the arts can use their time for intensive work within their specialties.

TESTING IN THE ARTS

The topic of testing in the arts is always bound to stir up a lively debate. Using the presentations by Eisner (Chapter 3) and Newman (Chapter 5) as a point of departure, the delegates discussed teaching a general knowledge of movement, dance, and acting. From this approach, one could develop a series of rather sterile experiences that could lead to a paper-and-pencil, multiple-choice test based on Laban's BSER framework. While recognizing this as a possibility, it was strongly felt that pursuing this direction as an arts experience for all would be a huge mistake because the medium should be moving, doing, and/or performing. All children need rich opportunities to express themselves creatively through movement. They must be allowed to experience the medium as it was intended; those with personal idiosyncrasies (special talent in this area) will emerge in diachronic fashion over time. The best assessment for this is through processfolios or portfolios that could be personal records or video tapes of dance and movement involvement over the years.

PRESERVICE AND IN-SERVICE TRAINING

Because of the movement for reform in teacher education, many states are preparing teachers with specialization in a chosen content area. While this may make it more difficult to develop an interdisciplinary base, most teachers are open to new ideas that may include integrating the arts for more effective teaching of their own subject. There have been several attempts at interdisciplinary aesthetic education, as evidenced by the programs at the University of Wisconsin–River Falls and at the Ohio State University. However, some of these programs have had to be aborted because funding was cut and/or enrollment was low. Our group had several suggestions for in-service training of teachers for interdisciplinary work: Teacher planning periods could be used to generate ideas of common interest. Arts commission grants could be used to bring artists, musicians, and dancers into the schools to train teachers. Many universities give teachers fee waivers to take courses in exchange for working with student teachers; these waivers could be used to take courses in the visual, performing, and literary arts.

TEACHING STYLE

Kinesthetic/movement teaching does not have to be done nor is it always accomplished in a creative or artistic fashion. For example, one could teach any part of the BSER framework in a rather mechanical and direct fashion. Creative, expressive, artistic dance/movement, however, is taught through a process-oriented method that uses problem solving, discovery, and exploration.

EXAMPLES OF MODEL PROGRAMS

The best way to implement the arts in education is from a bottom-up rather than a top-down approach. This may be best exemplified through charter schools, as proposed by Albert Shanker (1988; see Chapter 7, this book) and in the magnet schools developing in school districts across the country. Examples are the Ashley River Creative Arts Elementary School in Charleston, South Carolina, described by Rose Maree Myers, principal, in Chapter 6, and a similar school in Huntsville, Alabama. These schools are cited because of the work of each of the dance teachers in them. Millicent Simmons, who teaches at the Huntsville school, has a children's dance company and is well known for her work with the National Dance Association. Laurie Rich of the Charleston school, along with David Grabowski of North Myrtle Beach Elementary School, are featured artists in a film, *Dance in Physical Education,* developed by the South Carolina Department of Education (1989) on the dance curriculum in elementary schools.

An article in the May/June 1989 issue of JOPERD (AAHPERD, 1989) highlights several states for their progressive work toward including dance in the public school curriculum. Readers are referred to the article to learn what their own states are doing and/or to use the good examples in efforts to upgrade the status of dance in their states.

References

AAHPERD. (1989). Dance Dynamics—An Update on States' Dance Curricula. *JO-PERD, 60* (5), 31–58.

Gardner, H. (1983). *Frames of mind: The theory of multiple intelligences.* New York: Basic Books.

Gim, J. M. (1989). *Physical education as artful knowing.* Unpublished doctoral dissertation, Ohio State University, Columbus.

H'Doubler, Margaret. (1966). *Dance: A creative art experience.* Madison: University of Wisconsin Press.

Kern, S. (1983). *The culture of time and space, 1880–1918.* London: Weidenfelf and Nicolson, Ltd.

Shanker, A. (1988, July 10). Convention plots new course—a charter for change. *The New York Times,* p. E–7.

South Carolina Department of Education. (1989). *Dance in physical education* [Film]. Copies are available through Ruth Earls at the state Department of Education, Columbia, SC 29201.

World of the studio. (1989, March). *Brooklyn College Magazine* (City University of New York), *5,* pp. 12–13.

11 MUSIC

Artistic Intelligences and Music Education

CHARLES R. HOFFER

By now, it is clear that the idea of different intelligences and aptitudes is a well-accepted one, at least among the authors of this book. It has been recognized in music since at least the days of Carl Seashore in his Measures of Musical Talents test, developed in the early part of this century (Seashore, 1919). Seashore resisted the idea of combining the six subtests of his efforts into a single score, preferring to indicate that these were six somewhat independent musical talents. Guilford's Structure of the Intellect also supports the idea of different aspects of intelligence, and that model of the intellect has also been around since at least 1967 (Guilford, 1967; Guilford & Hoepfner, 1971).

My contribution would seem to be to offer some thoughts on what this means for the teaching of music. I would like to explore two particular aspects of the question: first, the relationship of attitudes and musical ability, and second, the nature of what is commonly referred to as "talent" or "aptitude" in music itself.

ATTITUDES AND MUSICAL ABILITY

Questions about interest and ability are fascinating. Does ability cause one to develop an interest in a particular area, or is it more likely that interest leads to the development of ability? Clearly, no one knows precisely, but it appears probable that one does influence the other. Which comes first is as difficult to determine as the proverbial "chicken/egg" question. It is only human to continue to do things for which one receives recognition, especially when one realizes that his or her efforts are better than those of most other people. If I were good at bowling—consistently bowling 200 or higher—then I would like to go bowling. The very fact that I bowl frequently would help me to become a better bowler. (By the way, I am *not* a good bowler!) On the other hand, activities that one does not do well are usually avoided, if at all possible. None of us likes to be in a situation in which we are made to look bad or feel incompetent.

The determination of that relationship leads to a further question: From where do interests come? This is an even more complex matter. There are some rather interesting theories about the formation of attitudes and interests. One theory is that they are learned through a process of association and reinforcement. This relates to the preceding point. For example, a student who wins a medal for playing a trumpet solo will have his or her interest furthered and promoted much more than a student who does not do well. In addition, the student who wins the medal for playing the trumpet will have far more pleasant associations with the instrument than will the student who "blew it."

A second view holds that interests are often determined by actions that maximize a person's benefits, somewhat the idea of "when in Rome, do as the Romans do." If it is beneficial to play trumpet well, then that is a spur to interest; if it is not beneficial to oneself, that certainly has a chilling effect on interest. It is easy to observe instances of this in high school sports. Students will display an enormous interest and undergo terrific hardship to be successful in certain sports because the psychological rewards in terms of public attention and potential economic rewards are so great. Take away those rewards, and I suspect that the interest in the particular sport would wane drastically.

A third view of the development of interest is that people seek consistency in what they encounter and dislike things that don't seem to fit. People are bothered by music that they can't understand and that doesn't agree with their preconceived notions of what music should be. I suspect this happens with tone row and other avant-garde music. It makes us feel a bit incompetent, because we feel that somehow we should be able to understand it.

Interests are spurred on by knowledge and familiarity. It is very difficult for me to become interested in a cricket match. I simply don't know what is happening in cricket. (And I suspect that even some Englishmen who watch cricket don't fully understand it!) Maybe it's exciting, but maybe it is not. In either case, it doesn't matter much because I don't understand what is taking place. Now, perhaps if I had knowledge of cricket, then I might become as excited as most Englishmen do at a good cricket match. Such knowledge would cause me to appear socially more "in the know," thereby providing the reward of self-enhancement as well.

What are some of the implications of the way attitudes are formed for instruction in music? One is that interests are something that cannot be taught directly. The old saying is, "Attitudes are caught, not taught." Interests are picked up in a variety of ways, often by modeling someone who is admired or in some activity that seems especially attractive to the person. It also implies that a situation in which instruction takes place should be one with a pleasant, positive atmosphere. A few students will withstand all sorts of carping criticism and still continue an interest in music. However, most students will avoid activities that bring a great deal of unhappiness and frustration.

Granted, positive and pleasant experiences are desirable, and attitudes of success promote interest, which in turn seems to encourage greater achievement. This raises important questions for music educators: If there are different intelligences among people, can everyone succeed at music? Can everyone become truly educated in music? If so, to what extent? Clearly, not everybody is going to achieve a high level of technical skill on piano or violin. If that were to happen, then we would need to redefine what we mean by "highly skilled." We would have to make some distinctions such as "very high" and "not so high."

What does seem more practical is to teach as though nearly everyone can achieve a level of competence at which music is meaningful and enjoyable. By this, I mean such tasks as being able to sing a simple song in a reasonably accurate manner and to listen intelligently to a Mozart symphony. While not everybody can achieve such a level, it does appear within reach for most students, if they are provided a quality education in music. Clearly, some students will go far beyond this level. However, music educators need to consider the many students who will not achieve high levels of technical and listening skill, as well as those who will.

MUSICAL APTITUDE

The second matter I wish to explore is the murky question of musical ability. This question has interested psychologists and educators at least since the beginning of this century. There is even considerable debate over which term to use. Radocy and Boyle (1979) suggest that the terms *talent* and *musicality* are not precise enough. They prefer the term *musical capacity* when referring to genetic endowment. They recommend that *musical aptitude* be used to refer to genetic ability plus informal environmental factors, plus formal instruction.

Not only is the matter one of definition, but it is probably far more complex than we like to admit. Perhaps Seashore was right when, in his Measures of Musical Talents, he did not want the six scores averaged (Seashore et al., 1960). Nor did his test include many of the aspects of music; in fact, the sounds of the test are distinctly unmusical to most people. But over the years, the idea of testing for inborn capacity for making music has intrigued psychologists and others, and many different approaches have been attempted.

The concept of musical ability is further complicated because the inborn capacity of processing auditory information is only a small part of musicianship. Most of us are familiar with stereotypes about some musicians: the good singer who can hardly pass music theory courses and the scholarly oboe player who is unsuccessful when attempting to lead a group. Indeed, throughout music history, there have been examples of well-known musicians who seemed to possess certain aspects of musical talent, while at the same time being quite unsuccessful in other ways. One was Tchaikovsky, who nearly ruined the premiere of his Sixth Symphony because he was such a poor conductor. Chopin was a great composer for piano, but he seemed either uninterested or unsuccessful in writing for any other medium. The same can be said for composers such as Wieniawski, who was highly successful in writing for the violin; Popper, who composed many works for the cello; Hugo Wolf, who is an important composer of art songs; and others who seemed to confine their efforts to only one area of music.

When one thinks of innate musical ability, Mozart comes to mind first. For him, writing music seemed extremely easy; his manuscripts seldom contained any changes and look very neat. Beethoven, on the other hand, found some of his music difficult to compose, especially vocal works, like his opera *Fidelio*. Some of his manuscripts look like a massive struggle took place on them. Does this mean that Mozart was talented and Beethoven was not? Clearly, I am not prepared to say that Beethoven was not talented, even if composing required much greater effort than it did for Mozart!

Often musical ability is coupled with other abilities in particular situations. For example, to be a successful opera singer, one needs to have not only a powerful voice that is reasonably accurate in terms of pitch and other factors, but also a certain sense of stage presence and acting ability. It is not possible to be successful in opera today by just standing there singing. Some people who are quite talented performing in an orchestral situation (e.g., the scholarly oboe player) would be hopelessly lost on stage attempting to project a song. On the other hand, one may be able to do arrangements, compose, play in an orchestra, and in other ways be successful in music without possessing much stage presence.

The subject becomes even more intriguing if we consider some "what if" circumstances. Assuming that he were still alive, suppose that Louis

Armstrong were to attempt to get into a major music school today. I wonder if he could do so. Even if he had learned how to read music, he would not have been admitted as a voice major. Whether he would have been willing to expend the effort to learn to play some of the difficult solo literature for the trumpet can be guessed at, but no one knows. On the other hand, he definitely possessed a monumental ability for utilizing and processing certain styles of music and for improvising on basic chord patterns. Was Louis Armstrong talented in some ways? Obviously, the answer is yes. Was he more talented than other trumpet players? That would depend on the kind of music being played. Was he talented in all areas of music? Obviously not.

IMPLICATIONS FOR TEACHING MUSIC

I have mentioned some past, present, and potential situations because I wish to make the point that the concept of differing intelligences probably not only refers to the arts versus science or verbal ability versus mechanical ability, and the like, but even divides a field like music into various subcategories. Music, it appears, should be thought of not as a monolithic ability but rather as an activity with a great variety of aspects. This means that music teachers should not teach all students in the same way or have the same expectations of all students. It suggests that students be provided a variety of opportunities. Some students should be encouraged to try to be top performers, while others should perhaps be encouraged to do other kinds of things in music, including careful listening. For others, maybe it is some activity like singing a simple tune with guitar accompaniment.

One of the unfortunate facts about music education today at the secondary school level is that we have tended to present only one type of music education: participation in performing organizations. The fact is that nearly 95 percent of all enrollments in high school music are in bands, choral groups, and orchestras. For students who are not interested in performance, there are usually no other opportunities available. Since most schools offer a rather limited music program, either a student performs or he or she doesn't take music.

An attempt is being made today to develop other kinds of music for high school students. Part of this attempt has not come from the profession of music education but rather has been thrust upon music teachers or offered to them (depending on how we look at it) by the actions of various state legislatures and state boards of education. Today, about 28 states require that students take some type of fine arts for graduation from high school. This situation offers music teachers an opportunity they have not had before to reach a far greater number of students. The problem is that most of these students are not going to fall into the traditional mold of learning to play an instrument or to sing. They require a different approach to music because their interests and abilities are different. Whether music educators take advantage of or fumble this opportunity will depend partly on their attitude toward teaching students who do not possess the traditional orientation toward performing. In any case, music teachers need to think about the different interests and intelligences of students.

The concept of different intelligences and approaches to music is certainly a useful and important one. It has more implications than I have explored here. What I have discussed is a beginning, and the questions raised are something that music educators need to consider seriously.

Comments on Music Education

CHARLES ELLIOTT

Debate in Western culture regarding the role of the arts in the education of the young can be traced back at least as far as the ancient Greeks. Plato suggested that the ideal system of education should focus on music and gymnastics (Mark, 1986). Since that time, the importance placed upon the arts in education has waxed and waned depending on the particular educational philosophy in vogue.

When music was introduced into the public schools of this country in 1838, its role was considered to be primarily recreational and peripheral to the central task of schooling, that of teaching the basic reading and writing skills. A part of the function of music in that setting was to serve as a break from the rigors of the school day (Birge, 1966).

Since 1838, the arguments made by music educators for the inclusion of music in the school curriculum have changed regularly in order to conform to changing educational philosophies. Because the rationale offered by the music education profession for including music in the curriculum has been changed and revised so often, some have accused music educators of being "bandwagon jumpers." There is, perhaps, some justification in that charge. While we as a profession have been quick to revise what we consider to be our "philosophy of music education," rarely have we been willing to wage an all-out battle for what we think should be the aim of public education in general. The widespread discussion generated by Howard Gardner's (1983) theory of multiple intelligences and the interest shown by educators from a variety of disciplines are perhaps signs that this reticence on the part of music educators, and arts educators in general, is about to change. The basic argument should not be whether or not music (or any other subject, for that matter) should be included in the school curriculum. Rather, it should address issues related to the aims and purposes of our public education system in general and whether or not that system is really intended to serve the needs of *all* the youth of the United States.

CONTENT-CENTERED VERSUS CHILD-CENTERED PHILOSOPHIES

An examination of the various educational philosophies that have held sway in this country during the past century-and-a-half will show that each can be placed in one of two categories—content centered or child centered. Those that espouse the content-centered view propose that there should be a predetermined curriculum that all children should be required to complete. This view is also usually characterized by an emphasis on standardized testing, a rigid and traditional curriculum with few electives, and the willingness to accept a high failure rate among students. The content of the curriculum during these periods can become a hot political issue and is usually determined, or at least greatly influenced, by those who hold economic power. The task of schooling, therefore, becomes that of molding the child to the curriculum. Much of the educational reform that has taken place in this country in recent years strongly reflects this content-centered view.

The child-centered view is based upon the premise that no two children are alike and that the curriculum should reflect those individual differences. This view is usually characterized by a flexible curriculum, nontraditional course offerings, numerous electives, a de-emphasis on standardized testing, and a low failure rate among students. The purpose of schooling thus becomes that of molding the curriculum to the needs of the individual child. The child-centered philosophy of education usually holds sway during periods of social reform, such as that which took place in this country during the late 1960s. Critics of this view argue, with some justification, that during periods when this philosophy is in vogue such basic skills as reading and math computation usually suffer a decline. Suffice it to say that those courses considered by many to be "nontraditional," such as the arts, flourish during those periods when the emphasis is on child-centered education and decline when content-centered education is in vogue.

Howard Gardner's (1983) theory of multiple intelligences, if it becomes widely accepted, will likely result in a return in this country to a more child-centered approach to public education than has been the case in the past decade. Gardner's theory, however, has an added advantage— it calls for fundamental philosophical reform in public education *based on scientific evidence,* a consideration rare in most educational reform.

REFORM OF PUBLIC SCHOOL MUSIC

If Gardner's theory does become widely accepted and the concomitant educational reform does occur, the implications for public school music could be profound. Gardner argues that musical intelligence is an entity separate from other forms of intelligence, that it usually emerges earlier than any of the other intelligences, and that in order for it to develop it must be nurtured rather early in life. There is evidence to show that in most instances the development of individual musical ability among the youth of this country is less a result of what happens in the public schools and more a result of the home environment (Rainbow, 1965). This raises the question, of course, as to how many children are being "lost" because of a failure of our public school system—children who given the opportunity could develop their special gifts and grow up to lead productive and rewarding lives. Gardner (1983) writes:

> In speaking of musically talented children, I am concerned with a tiny group of children who have been singled out by their families and their communities. *It is not known to what extent this number could be significantly increased were values and training methods to change.* (p. 112, emphasis added)

Gardner goes on to cite the example of S. Suzuki, who has demonstrated that it is possible for large numbers of individuals to become quite proficient at music even at an early age and that "such fluency is a reasonable target for a much larger proportion of the population than is currently the case in the United States" (p. 112).

Consideration should be given, however, to the descriptor *musical fluency* as used by Gardner. Does it refer simply to the ability to perform music? Can one be musically fluent without being a performer? What is the nature of musical ability? Do multiple musical intelligences exist? These are only a few of the questions that the music education profession will have to consider as Gardner's theory of multiple intelligences becomes more widely accepted by professional educators and the general public.

The type of educational reform implied by Gardner's theory should be welcomed by music educators. Such reform would likely result in the arts' being placed in a more secure position once again in public education. However, in order to ensure that the gains made for arts education under such a reform will survive the inevitable swing in the pendulum back toward a more content-centered philosophy, music educators should heed some of the warnings from past mistakes and practices and begin a reform movement in public school music, something that is long overdue.

The serious study of music, and indeed all the arts, is as difficult as the study of any discipline. Unfortunately, few public school music programs offer a sequential and rigorous course of study such as that offered in other disciplines. The music education profession should initiate a reform movement to rectify this. Students who have the talent (Gardner would say intelligence) and the desire to pursue a serious study of music should be provided that opportunity during their public school years. At the present time, students who elect to study music seriously usually do so after school hours at their own expense. Those who cannot afford such study or who live in areas where such after-school resources are not available are usually deprived of those opportunities. For those students, the claim that American public education is meant to serve the needs of the individual and that it affords all children an equal opportunity certainly takes on a hollow ring. Though Gardner calls for reform that would make such opportunities available, few public school music programs are structured so that they could provide those opportunities if called upon to do so.

In addition to the need for curricular reform, consideration must also be given to the task of identifying those children with exceptional musical ability. The procedures typically used now are notoriously unreliable, especially in dealing with younger children. At present, research seems to indicate that reliance on a single test score, regardless of the test, is not advisable. The most effective procedures seem to employ a profile or a portfolio of some kind. Needless to say, such procedures can be time-consuming and are also themselves not infallible. Therefore, while the music education profession should support Gardner's call for reform, it should also take the steps necessary to get its own house in order. There is much research and work yet to be done.

Finally, one caveat is in order. Music educators have long argued that music should be a part of the general education of all children and that the opportunity should be available for everyone to make music a part of their lives. The danger exists that, should widespread educational reform occur in light of Gardner's theory, an emphasis will be placed on the musical education of only that small percentage of students who are identified as having exceptional ability. Such a development would be the antithesis of every rationale and philosophy offered for American public school music over the past 150 years.

References

Birge, E. B. (1966). *History of public school music in the United States.* Washington, DC: Music Educators National Conference.

Gardner, H. (1983). *Frames of mind: The theory of multiple intelligences.* New York: Basic Books.

Guilford, J. P. (1967). *The nature of human intelligence.* New York: McGraw-Hill.

Guilford, J. P., & Hoepfner, R. (1971). *The analysis of intelligence.* New York: McGraw-Hill.

Mark, M. L. (1986). *Contemporary music education.* New York: Schirmer Books.

Radocy, R. E., & Boyle, J., Jr. (1979). *Psychological foundations of musical behavior.* Springfield, IL: Charles C. Thomas.

Rainbow, E. L. (1965). A pilot study to investigate the constructs of musical aptitude. *Journal of Research in Music Education, 13,* 3–14.

Seashore, C. E. (1919). *Seashore Measures of Musical Talent.* New York: Columbia Phonograph Company.

Seashore, C. E., Lewis, L., & Saetveit, J. G. (1960). *Seashore Measures of Musical Talents.* New York: Psychological Corporation.

Part IV

RECAPITULATION

In this part the main themes of the book return, but, unlike in a musical composition, there are new insights. In Chapter 12, Maxine Greene uses words to embody the spirit of aesthetic education and, in that way, gives form to the changes envisioned in this book.

Charles Fowler, in Chapter 13, epitomizes the contents and spirit of the preceding chapters, and he reminds us of the precarious position of the arts in education. Chapter 14 is a summary of salient points from the book in an effort to draw together the views of 20 writers.

12

Arts Education in the Humanities: Toward a Breaking of the Boundaries

Maxine Greene

It is invigorating and energizing to be asked to think and talk about the arts in South Carolina in early spring. I have been reminded in the last few days that human beings can have aesthetic experiences on the roads and in the woods, as well as in theatres, galleries, libraries, and concert halls. Burgeoning leaves, sudden glints of color, the sparkle of a lake viewed from a plane: all these can give pleasure, instants of insight, a consciousness of something disclosed. If asked, many of us might associate such experiences with what we feel (or intuit, or discover) during significant encounters with art forms. Much depends, I know, on how sensitive we are to the qualities of things, or to the look and sound of the appearing world. I wonder about the degree to which such awareness is gained through acquaintance with the arts. I wonder if we really know how to characterize such awareness, how we know when those we teach have attained it. Why does it seem so absolutely essential to some of us in times like these—in the midst of a demanding technological society and in relation to what Henry James called the "money grope"? Why do we argue for the centrality of the arts in schools and colleges at a time of so much insistence that what we really need is training to maintain the nation's economic competitiveness? Why do we emphasize the intrinsic value of the arts so much when most of us recognize the impacts of commodification and consumerism even on galleries, museums, opera companies, and so-called "serious" publishing houses? Why do we presume the value of a search for meaning and new perspectives at a moment when those in leadership keep stressing a return to the traditional? How, in any case, are we to meet the challenges of fundamentalism on the one hand and popular culture on the other?

147

We all, I am sure, are deeply interested in moving as many people as we can to pose their own questions in these domains. We also hope, I believe, that people will pose as many questions as they conceivably can about the arts and what they signify, and the difference they have made and can make in diverse human lives. To be complacent, to take for granted that we are on the side of the humane, the well-meaning, the cultivated, may be to give up the passion and the sense of mystery that keep fascination with the arts alive. An argument for consideration of aesthetics is that it may keep the troubling questions open. If they *are* open, the interrogative stance, the wonder, and the curiosity remain.

Aesthetics as a study takes shape, after all, in response to the most deeply felt questions human beings have raised with regard to their encounters with works of art. The oldest ones, of course, have to do with art's relation to cosmic reality or to some higher order of things. We need only recall Aristotle's *Poetics* (1947) and his talk of Tragedy as involving "the imitation of the *form* of action" (p. 637). Later questions, of more moment today, have to do with representation and expressiveness. To what degree does a Rembrandt self-portrait truly render the painter at a particular stage of his life? Does a Mahler song give expression to the composer's actual grief? Or has the song (like Martha Graham's "Lamentations" or Coleridge's "Ode to Dejection") been forged in a context of meanings that allowed the artist to give expression to feelings of which (despite pain) he or she may have been only dimly aware? Is it the song that over time gives content to the grief?

What *is* it about Auden's lines on Icarus ("a boy falling out of the sky") or Edward Hopper's desolate city streets or Picasso's exhausted woman ironing in a grey-brown world, that can touch us across the distances, make us see and feel as we may never have seen or felt before? What is it about the ending of *King Lear* or the killing of the child in Toni Morrison's *Beloved* that may feed our desire to live and to see rather than discourage us so much that we play with thoughts of suicide? Why do we choose such experiences, as devastating as some of them are? Is it really the case that the more we know about the formed content we are encountering, the more we can see and imagine and feel? I want persons to ask such questions because I believe that those who can communicate the sense that they have been personally and wonderingly present to works of art, are the ones most likely to arouse others to go in search, to wonder in their own fashions, to attend. I believe we need continually to suggest to others the ways in which we throb with forever unanswered (and perhaps unanswerable) questions, and the sense in which our preoccupation with the arts is as inexhaustible as the arts themselves. Doing so, we may find ourselves developing paradigms for learning, even for understanding. It is not sufficient, after all, to "know about." What is essential is to come to understand, to witness works of art with our lives.

There is so much that is mysterious in the quest for a means of opening other human beings to what may (or may not) move them to see and to hear. It is easy enough to affirm that we hope to enable them to perceive in such a manner that they will discover the expansion and intensification of experience that many people associate with aesthetic encounters. It is even easy enough to tell others that art forms are privileged objects, in the sense of being deliberately made to evoke the responses randomly aroused by leaves, branches, sunsets, children's voices in the everyday world. Privileged objects, for me, include paintings, sculptures, poems, novels, plays, musical pieces, and dance performances, with unique capacities to complicate and deepen our experiences in the world and with each other. They have the potential as well to plunge us into adventures of meaning and to open new perspectives on an always problematic world.

"My task," wrote Joseph Conrad (1960), "is to make you hear, to make you feel, to make you see. That, and no more, and it is everything. If I succeed, you shall find there according to your deserts: encouragement, consolation, fear, charm—all you demand—and, perhaps, also that glimpse of truth for which you have forgotten to ask" (pp. 30–31). That task is seldom done if people are not enabled to notice what there is to be noticed in a work, if they are not provoked to release their perceptual capacities, if they are not encouraged to let their imaginations move them into another experiential space. Imagination, after all, is the capacity to move beyond to what is not yet, to what might be; it is the capacity to break through the boundaries. I want to find out what can be done to help diverse persons see what there is for them in Winslow Homer's visions of the Maine coast—beyond the surf and the slickers and the darkness— what there is for them in Goya's "Disasters of War" in these times. What awaits them in Cezanne's "Lac d'Annecy" as the artist chose to feel it, shape it, show it? What do Picasso's images of pain, those fragments and interconnections, communicate in the "Guernica"? What of the Bach Cantatas, Schubert's "Trout Quintet"? We could go on to the ballet *Giselle,* to the South African theatre piece called *Sarafina,* to O'Neill's *Desire Under the Elms.* There are sea chanties to recall, and spirituals. There is Hawthorne's *The Scarlet Letter* (the created spaces of which still cry out for exploration) now provoking questions about nature and culture, sexuality and self-control, women and the new world required for their coming into their own. There is *Beloved,* mentioned earlier, a book that has disclosed for me not only images of what slavery was like in its concreteness, but what motherhood is like when you know you might lose your children, when you are always on the edge of an abyss.

Yes, all these communicate in different languages. They belong to different symbol systems—these depictions and kinetic patterns and soundings and sayings (Goodman, 1976). But they are all thought to belong to art worlds, and they each require a particular mode of grasping and attending. The quality of that attending may be enhanced by involving the beholder or the listener or the reader with a medium like that which has been transformed by Bach, say, or Cezanne, or Hartley, or Morrison. I have in mind, of course, the provision of opportunities for people to go in search of their own imagery, to work with shapes and color relationships, to try to transfigure their own commonplaces into something never seen on earth before. I can remember trying something like that when I was young, as can many other people. I remember saving words I especially esteemed: porcelain, moonlight, carnelian. And I remember thinking that, if I could only put them together somehow, they would do magic to the kitchen table where we ate cereal in the mornings, and where sunlight sometimes slid around the shade to light up the dull, familiar pitcher and the orange juice glasses and the left-over cereal. I thought the right words would change that ordinary scene into something different, light it somehow, make me find out how I really felt about it all. When I was a bit older, I tried to figure out how the published poets did it—in my time, Amy Lowell, Edna St. Vincent Millay. Couldn't *I* too be quiet and merry and ride "back and forth all night on the ferry"? (Millay, 1923, p. 340). They fed back and forth: my own trying to say, and my growing wonder at what a poet could say. I wondered wildly at the metaphors I found, the shaping of words, the music of them. Even today, when I find my world being profoundly altered by certain poets, I suspect it is because of not only what they can do but what I have struggled (usually unsuccessfully) to do. Still, I am glad I have tried; the effort to embody my emotions, my perceptions, into a made thing, an unreal world, a poem, has opened me to what is entailed by the making of a poem. I wish I could quote at length Elizabeth Bishop's (1983) "In the Waiting Room," that poem about the poet as remembered child waiting while her aunt has her teeth fixed in a dentist's office. What could be more ordinary—going to the dentist in Worcester, Massachusetts, on a dark winter afternoon? She reads *National Geographic* and sees on the pages naked women with breasts; she hears her aunt cry out in pain; she reminds herself she is almost seven.

> I was saying it to stop
> the sensation of falling off
> the round, turning world
> into cold, blue-black space.
> But I felt: you are an *I*,

you are an *Elizabeth*,
you are one of *them*.
Why should you be one, too? (p. 160)

The doors are opening for her into adulthood, into identity, into the thoughts of big black waves.

To explore our own language, to try to construct a world (as Elizabeth Bishop did) with our own pigments or sounds or gestures or words, is to come to understand art-making in some fashion, to grasp "making" itself. We may come intimately to grasp that those works called works of art do not spring fully fledged from the head or hands of artists to pages, canvasses, staffs, theatre spaces. We may begin to realize as well the ways in which we can discover our own sensations of falling off the world by writing them, by embodying them in language, just as we may discover the way the curve of the rock or the blaze of the red leaf discloses itself when we try to render it. Knowing this, I believe persons are more likely to grasp the idea that they must move beyond the stance of mere spectator or consumer if they are to come into the presence of works of art. They must become active in their looking and listening, conscious of themselves perceiving, aware of themselves striving to say and to see.

John Dewey's words rise up for me. In *Art as Experience* (1934), he reminded his readers how foolish it was to treat aesthetic perception as an affair for odd moments, and how likely many people are to confuse aesthetic perception with mere recognition: the attachment of the correct labels or titles to the Bishop poem or the Rembrandt portrait. In order to perceive fully, he said, beholders have to create their own experiences, since, without acts of recreation, objects could not be perceived as works of art. He did not mean trying to become a Bishop or a Rembrandt, or actually repainting a picture or reshaping a poem. He was reminding his readers that words printed on a page or mere strokes of paint on canvas do not automatically become aesthetic objects. The imaginative and perceptual energies of people who come to them must reach toward them if they are to be transmuted into a rendering of an aged Rembrandt or a little girl in a waiting room worried about falling off the world.

We tend to assume that the Rembrandt and the Bishop, no matter what the circumstances, are works of art. Perhaps it is more accurate to think of them as reservoirs of possibility, potential sources of aesthetic experience for those who know how to attend. Dewey (1934) wrote

There is work done on the part of the percipient as there is on the part of the artist. The one who is too lazy, idle, or indurated in convention to perform this work will not see or hear. His "appreciation" will be a mixture of scraps of learning with conformity to norms of conventional admiration and with a confused, even if genuine, emotional excitation. (p. 54)

I would stress those words—*lazy, idle, indurated*—because of the way they challenge passivity and mere receptivity. Also, the very term *indurated* connotes a hardening process, a petrifying process. We see people caught in convention in such a fashion that they cannot see alternatives, cannot look at things as if they could be otherwise, cannot (in Conrad's sense) "see."

This happens, as we are all aware, to numerous teachers under the conditions that now prevail in American public schools. Their fixity or their "induration" in convention or propriety or single-stranded prescriptions can only undermine the exploratory co-learning that provokes the young to move out on their own quests. And their quests must entail their own achievement of meanings, their own achievement of significance when it comes to works of art. We who are teachers can point to details of formed content; we can make metaphors visible; we can admonish when it comes to confusion between commonsense and illusioned worlds. We can open pathways to the study of social contexts, of styles, of horizons, of representation in its problematic complexity, of moments of "extraordinary particularity" (Berger, 1984, p. 61) that release us in novel ways to see. But we cannot impose an aesthetic experience upon another; we cannot legislate an aesthetic object into being for another's consciousness. We cannot instruct another what he or she is to perceive—hear, read, see.

Aesthetic education involves intentional efforts to nurture more and more informed awareness of various works of art. The aesthetic educator understands that the more the beholder can come to notice and to know, the more he or she is likely to hear and see, the wider will be what Martin Heidegger (1971) called the "clearing" in his or her consciousness (p. 53), the greater the likelihood of "unconcealment." But the clearing or the opening depends on the beholder's attentiveness. It depends on the degree to which he or she can uncouple from the mundane and the ordinary and allow his or her energies to pour into a work in order to bring it alive. If it were the case that works of art, especially those considered "great," opened themselves spontaneously to anyone passing by (or skimming the pages, or hearing a melody in the hall), we would not need anything like aesthetic education. We would not need it if we believed human beings possessed an inborn capacity to intuit what artists are trying to say, or what Ernst Gombrich (1960) called an "innocent eye" (p. 14), free enough of past experience and influence to see with absolute purity what an artist intends. We would not need it if so many works had not been withdrawn into protected enclaves, ascribed an aura, defined by Walter Benjamin (1978) as "the unique phenomenon of a distance" (p. 222). He meant that works of art were presented as in some sense ideal forms, belonging to an objectively timeless realm, out of reach of the ordinary woman or man. Like Dewey's (1934) discussion of works of art losing their roots in lived cultural life and becoming "specimens of fine art and nothing else" (p. 9), Benjamin's was meant to call attention to the importance of helping people cross the established distances, crack the ostensibly esoteric codes, appropriate what was worth appropriating as human beings with equal rights in the world. Because of the persistence of such distancing and such mystification, aesthetic education may function to demystify, to break through barriers and bars. Today, these include commodification, the "hype," the various modes of consumerism. By encouraging a critical as well as an appreciative consciousness, aesthetic education can release persons in often unexpected ways. But, again, much depends upon the teacher's own restlessness and reflectiveness, upon his or her ability to keep the questions burning and alive, even as the clearings open and the possibilities of aesthetic pleasure increase.

Denis Donoghue (1983) has written about the sense in which the arts can be "really momentous, because they provide for spaces in which we can live in total freedom" (p. 129). He means spaces in which we do not coincide with our "ordinary selves" or conform to convention, routine, and habit most of the time. And then

> The arts are on the margin, and it doesn't bother me to say that they are marginal. What bothers me is the absurd claims we make for them. I want to say that the margin is the place for those feelings and intuitions which daily life doesn't have a place for and mostly seems to suppress. And the most important intuition is of mystery. . . . Even in a world mostly secular, the arts can make a space for our intuition of mystery, which isn't at all the same thing as saying that the arts are a substitute for religion. . . . In art, faith doesn't arise. It's enough that the arts have a special care for those feelings and intuitions which otherwise are crowded out in our works and days. With the arts, people can make a space for themselves, and fill it with intimations of freedom and presence. (p. 129)

The arts cannot be fully explicated or explained, in general or in their particularity. Presently, they may be in danger of being drained of their power by "cherishing" bureaucracies, according to Donoghue. They may be made instrumental to extrinsic ends (or purposes defined by people with interests at odds with the "feelings and intuitions . . . otherwise . . .

crowded out," ends subsumed under concepts like "civilization" or "cultural literacy." It is the work of books like this and of those who do aesthetic education to rediscover and reaffirm what resists reductionism in the arts today, what opens to possibility. I cannot but turn to Wallace Stevens (1982) for imagery that suggests far better than discourse what this might mean. This is the last stanza of his "Six Significant Landscapes":

> Rationalists, wearing square hats,
> Think in square rooms,
> Looking at the floor,
> Looking at the ceiling.
> They confine themselves
> To right-angled triangles.
> If they tried rhomboids,
> Cones, waving ellipses—
> As for example, the ellipse of the half moon—
> Rationalists would wear sombreros. (p. 75)

Clearly, it does not suggest the obliteration of rationalists or the mode of linear, logical thinking they are committed to do. But it does evoke images of change and expansion, yes, of transformation. There is a glimpse of an alternative reality; even rationalists may choose to go beyond mere coinciding with their rationalist selves. Such a view may subvert ordinary petrified "reality." But it opens to the untapped and the unrealized; it may, to those who accept the risk, "unconceal."

The point has to do not only with breaking with confinement to a single mode of knowing, a single room. It has to do with being able to become aware of the possibility of multiple realities. Maurice Merleau-Ponty (1964) once wrote

> Vision is not a certain mode of thought or presence to self; it is the means given me for being absent from myself, for being present at the fission of Being from the inside—the fission at whose termination, and not before, I come back to myself. (p. 186)

He had in mind the self-development of the artist, of the contexts of meaning in which such a person struggles to find a vision. We might summon up Matisse's painting called "The Red Studio," which includes images the artist had created over time, a pictorial history of his struggle to "see" in his own fashion. To develop a vision meant to challenge accepted ways of interpreting reality, to enable those who would come to his paintings to see in accord with them, to see things in new ways. Sometimes, as in the case of the sudden appearance of Manet's "Luncheon on the Grass" at the Salon des Refusés in Paris, people are shocked because of the way the vantage point diverges from ordinary ways of constructing reality and even human relationships. The same thing might be said of Gustave Flaubert's *Madame Bovary* and Charles Baudelaire's *Flowers of Evil,* not to speak of Fyodor Dostoevsky's *Notes from Underground.* Herman Melville's *Moby Dick,* as is well known, was shunned for three-quarters of a century after its publication. Brahm's music, like Stravinsky's, was mocked and booed.

But our hope is to summon persons, even within the public schools, away from "the already constituted reason," to release them to come in touch with their own visions, with their own lived lives in which, after all, their reason originates. Perhaps oddly, this is most likely to happen when new perspectives can be opened on experience. And I would want to stress again that encounters with the arts can open such perspectives if people take the time to be personally present to diverse works, to weave circles of quietness in which they can meet a painting or a poem or a work of music as if they were meeting another human being with an energy waiting to be expressed. Personal presentness of this kind, however, does not have to signify a total autonomy or a totally private meeting with a Cezanne, a Hartley, a Martha Graham, a Virginia Woolf. We are, after all, all members of some human community. We would not be persons were it not for having grown up within some network of communication and relationship. We exist in the medium of a social reality, an interpreted complex of experiences constructed by ourselves, our predecessors, and our contemporaries. The works we encounter, no matter how *avant-garde* or how disruptive of our certainties, also belong to a web of relationships surrounding them in the present, extending back into the past. We become gradually aware of the ways in which present works make use of what Gombrich (1960) has called "cryptograms" (p. 39) invented in earlier times, codes, ways of contrasting flatness to deepness, of highlighting colors; ways of expressing tension in dance movement and resolution; ways of telling stories, extending tales into novels, transfiguring and yet making more intelligible the intersubjective world. Within the fabrics of the humanities, we ought to be able to communicate the sense of this ongoing, continuous effort to find human modes of saying and showing forth, of sounding and singing the multiple ways there have been of being in the world. Just because there have been and will continue to be multiple interpretations of every particular work, history itself keeps opening possibilities for further meaning. And these possibilities, as has been said, can be realized only if opportunities are provided for informed, personal engagement.

We know full well how much nostalgia exists for presumably lost unities, for some objectively existent stage in history when coherence could be recognized and achieved. We know how many are attempting to restore or impose a stability upon the young by concentrating on reclaiming what is called our "legacy," by reaffirming our heritage, by insisting on a kind of monologism rather than what is being called a "heteroglossia" (Bakhtin, 1971, p. 263), a phenomenon of many voices, multiple meanings. There are people calling for a return to the canonical, to "high art" in its most ancient meaning, having to do with eternality or something over-arching, lawful, and awe-inspiring like the "Ode to Joy" or the Sistine Chapel or the imagining of Dante's Paradise. The hope is to find a compelling metaphor for new transcendences, new reconciliations that will counter relativism and protect our world from vulgarity, sensationalism, and immorality. Some still will claim that the primary justification for including the arts in school curricula is that they allow the young to come in touch with the best ever thought and said by human beings (overlooking Bosch's paintings and *Tamburlaine* and *Richard III,* the de Sade fictions, and *The Gulag Peninsula*). It is said that the arts, well taught, provide occasions for reaching out toward the universal, the truly good, or to images of grandeur that might restore the soul. Others do not speak quite in that fashion, but do insist that our culture is crumbling and that, if we are to survive, we have to initiate the young into something coherent and enduring, identified with the truth of our heritage.

I am suggesting here that, for all the fears of relativism and idiosyncratic vision, we need to keep seeking for the clearings through which the young may be empowered to find their way. There are liberating effects to be sought in breaking with the taken-for-granted, in arousing ourselves from what Virginia Woolf (1976) called the "cotton wool of daily life" (p. 70), from banality and the kind of everydayness that make it harder and harder to learn. My concern is for wide-awakeness, for the capacity to perceive and reflect upon what is so frequently concealed by the familiar and the habitual, as well as by ignorance. And we have to argue for the arts, I believe, as more than decorative, more than sources of sensual delight, even as we argue for them as something other than exemplars of tradition, contributors to cultural literacy. Opening the kinds of spaces described, they may become occasions for survival in a world grown egocentric, privatistic, mean.

Of course, there is no guarantee that persons will be improved as moral beings because new horizons open; but, then, there never are guarantees. Among the consummations we may be entitled to hold in mind are the erosions of objectivism, of weary acquiescence to an unreflected-upon "real." Along with this may come a renewed perception of the role of human consciousness in the constitution of a range of meanings in addition to the achievement of diverse works of art. This kind of realization may launch teachers into new visions, a new sense of existential possibility for themselves and those they teach. Provoked to attentiveness, beginning to be authentically present to illusioned worlds in their particularity, they may be at least capable of looking at things as if they could be otherwise. Awakened to alternative possibility, alive to the uses of breaking through boundaries, their lives and expectations may be changed. Equally important may be the opportunity for them to see themselves as members of larger human communities—moving toward others as "who" rather than "what" they are, disclosing themselves through speech and action, as Hannah Arendt (1958) has said, constituting between them the beginnings of a common world.

The questions remain open. The dissonances remain. Those of us who are serious about art and the future will have to continue struggling against the determinates of the technical and economic world, the world of inattentiveness and violence and lack of care. We will have to struggle against disorder as well, and shiftlessness, and what one art critic has recently called "glitz and gleam." But we will be untrue to the message of the arts we are trying to make significant in diverse lives—the message that concludes one of Rainer Maria Rilke's (1958) poems—if we accede to mere conventionality, to petrification, to mystification. The message emerges at the end of a poem called "Torso of an Archaic Apollo"; and, as in the case of most poetry, it cannot be excised from the work itself.

Never will we know his fabulous head
Where the eyes' apples slowly ripened. Yet
His torso glows: a candelabrum set
Before his gaze which is pushed back and hid,

Restrained and shining. Else the curving breast
Could not thus blind you, nor through the soft turn
Of the loins could this smile easily have passed
Into the bright groins where the genitals burned.

Else stood this stone a fragment and defaced,
With lucent body from the shoulders falling,
Too short, not gleaming like a lion's fell;

Nor would this star have shaken the shackles off,
Bursting with light, until there is no place
That does not see you. You must change your life. (p. 93)

It is the message of the educator, the message of the artist: "You must change your life." In what direction? Why and how? The problem remains; the mystery pulls at us. How do we create situations that release the young to pay heed?

References

Arendt, H. (1958). *The human condition.* Chicago: University of Chicago Press.

Aristotle. (1947). *Poetics, introduction to Aristotle* (R. McKeon, Ed.). New York: Modern Library.

Bakhtin, M. M. (1971). *The dialogic imagination.* Austin: University of Texas Press.

Benjamin, W. (1978). *Illuminations.* New York: Schocken Books.

Berger, J. (1984). *Ways of seeing.* London: Pelican Books.

Bishop, E. (1983). *Collected poems.* New York: Farrar, Straus, Giroux.

Conrad, J. (1960). Preface to *The "Nigger" of the Narcissus.* In J. E. Miller, Jr. (Ed.), *Myth and method* (pp. 28–32). Lincoln: University of Nebraska Press.

Dewey, J. (1934). *Art as experience.* New York: Minton, Balch.

Donoghue, D. (1983). *The arts without mystery.* Boston: Little, Brown.

Gombrich, E. (1960). *Art and illusion.* New York: Pantheon Press.

Goodman, N. (1976). *Languages of art.* Indianapolis: Hackett Publishing.

Heidegger, M. (1971). *Poetry, language, and thought.* New York: Harper & Row.

Merleau-Ponty, M. (1964). Eye and mind. In *Primacy of perception* (pp. 159–190). Evanston: Northwestern University Press.

Millay, E. St. V. (1923). Recuerdo. In H. Monroe & A. C. Henderson (Eds.), *The new poetry* (p. 340). New York: Macmillan.

Rilke, R. M. (1958). *Selected poems* (C. F. MacIntyre, Trans.). Berkeley: University of California Press.

Stevens, W. (1982). *Collected poems.* New York: Vintage Books.

Woolf, V. (1976). *Moments of being: Unpublished autobiographical writings* (J. Schulkind, Ed.). New York: Harcourt, Brace & Jovanovich.

13

One Nation, Undercultured and Underqualified

CHARLES FOWLER

Those of us who have been around arts education for the past 30 to 40 years have to acknowledge that our progress has suffered from severe impediments. The arts have not prospered in American schools. Indeed, as I observed elsewhere (Fowler, 1988), the possible significance of the arts in the education of American youth is largely unrecognized, often ignored, and generally underrated. For the past decade, perhaps longer, arts programs in many American schools have been systematically dismantled. Access to the vast treasury of American and world culture is denied to many American children, with the result that their education is incomplete, their minds less enlightened, their lives less enlivened. In many of our largest cities, a downtrodden army of cultureless children is marching this civilization toward a new age of barbarism. The sheer number of these future citizens and their personal barrenness confront us with prospects of a diminishing cultural future: One nation, undercultured and underqualified. Is this the best we can do?

When I first read Howard Gardner's book *Frames of Mind* (1983), I was struck by how the arts seem to emanate from various discrete forms of intelligence: creative writing from linguistic intelligence; music from musical intelligence; visual arts from spatial intelligence; dance from bodily kinesthetic intelligence; and theatre from the personal intelligences. And I thought how the arts define the mind and the mind defines what education ought to be. But that is not the way education works, as Gardner reminds us. He says:

> Among those observers partial to spatial, bodily, or musical forms of knowing, as well as those who favor a focus on the interpersonal aspects of living, an inclination to indict contemporary schooling is under-

standable. The modern secular school has simply, though it need not have, neglected these aspects of intellectual competence. (p. 356)

I am tired of the arts being the underdogs in American education. I'm outraged by the neglect, and I've grown impatient with the indifference. But I think that much of the problem lies directly on the shoulders of arts educators and that *we* are the ones who have to initiate the changes if the arts are to attain greater education stature. I'd like to look at some of the reasons for this neglect and what we might do to alter the pattern.

EDUCATION FOR COMMERCE

I believe that the decline in the status of the arts started in 1957 with Russia's launching of Sputnik. Our response was a massive ($1 billion) federal mobilization of education to meet the pressing demands of national security and to maintain our competitive edge in math and science. This conscription of education to serve the nation's political and economic agenda set a precedent. In 1983, the federal report *A Nation at Risk* again tied education directly to our ability to compete in world markets and to regain "our once unchallenged preeminence in commerce, industry, science, and technological innovation" (National Commission on Excellence in Education, 1983, p. 5).

Roughly, this same 30-year period from 1957 to the present coincides with the beginning of the television age and the birth of the technological society. While television saturates us in superficial glitz and vacuous entertainment, technology demands deeper scientific knowledge and more highly specialized education. While the former lulls the mind to stupor, the latter urges it to new levels of literacy. Both of these opposing—or complementary—phenomena have had a serious, and largely deleterious, effect on arts education in public schools. The public tends to associate education in the arts with the frivolous world of TV and entertainment, not with the technological future that has become the serious business of education.

Exacerbating the situation is the further conscription of education to serve the interest of the corporate and business sectors. Hardly a week goes by without some corporate executive complaining about the quality of our educational system, and usually with good cause. Indeed, AT&T says it spends $6 million a year to educate 14,000 employees in basic reading and math. American Express claims it spends more than $10 million a year to teach its employees to do their jobs competently. Other corporations have also been forced to engage seriously with education. The report of the Committee for Economic Development (1985), which represents most of the major corporations in the United States, states that "our schools stand accused of failing the nation's children and leaving the economy vulnerable to better-educated and more highly trained international competitors" (p. 2).

What does business want? The committee's survey of the needs of industry reveals that they are looking for young people who demonstrate first of all "a sense of responsibility, self-discipline, pride, teamwork, and enthusiasm" (p. 17), and second the ability to learn, to solve problems, and to communicate well. Does the committee see any role for the arts in serving these educational interests? Yes, they acknowledge that the arts, which they call nonacademic extracurricular activities, are worthwhile for "certain students." Even though they admit that "music, drama, and art develop an appreciation of aesthetics and cultural awareness and require discipline and teamwork," they suggest that eligibility for participation be based on "a desired level of academic competence" (p. 22).

This shortsighted view has got to be corrected. It is a problem we have to solve. By underestimating the educational potential of the arts for every student, corporate leaders further relegate the arts to the educational periphery. It is up to us to remind these leaders that it is going to take more than the ability to read, write, and compute to make productive citizens. In fact, I think we need to make the case that what business wants of young people cannot be achieved *without* the arts and that they should want much more. But how do we make that case?

THE STATUS OF THE ARTS

The unrelenting pressure on schools to serve corporate and commercial needs has established an elite core of subjects in American schools that is labeled "the basics"—the subjects that every student must master. The arts are seldom admitted to the club. This shutout has aroused the arts education community. We want to know why the arts cannot command anything more than marginal status in the public educational system.

In 1985, the Getty Center for Education in the Arts launched a nationwide effort to make art education more academic, with the thought that increased rigor and a broader curriculum encompassing aesthetics, art history, and art criticism, as well as the development of the skills of production, would alter perceptions of art education and establish it as a basic. The center believes that, if we want it to be a basic subject, it has to look and act like one. That is what gains respect for a subject (Getty Center, 1985). These efforts are still underway. Clearly, finding the way to become basic is the central galvanizing issue in the field of arts education today.

What has kept the arts on the fringes of educational respectability? What keeps them from being basic? Is it that our educational and corporate leaders do not equate the arts with mentation? Probably. Is it that they do not associate the arts with the particular utilitarian abilities that they expect education to impart? Undoubtedly. The fundamental purpose of American schooling today, whether we agree with it or not, is preparation for work. We have been advised by Mary Futrell (see Chapter 4) to hold out against the tidal wave of the economic imperative, but are our economic problems a temporary malady? We must remember that schools have been serving the nation's economic agenda for at least 30 years. As educational priorities have shifted to serve the needs of commerce and international competition, the arts appear more and more frivolous—totally superfluous to those controlling purposes. This is the reality we face in the arts. Our arts electives are being replaced by computer science, more math, more English, more history—exactly what economic interests dictate. Many of our school systems have bought the idea of *A Nation at Risk.* That is why making study of the arts more serious and sequential or focused on the acquisition of knowledge, as the National Endowment for the Arts (1988) advocates, is not enough. Please note that I did not say it was wrong; it is just not enough. Simply being more intellectual and demanding about the way we teach the arts will not succeed in winning us basic status because the arts were not excluded on just that basis. They were excluded because, in light of the main purpose of education, they appear expendable, extraneous, and nonessential.

Corporations continue to demand that schools serve the narrow but very real goal of employability, and the arts continue to fail to connect—no matter how broad or intellectual their curriculum. Therefore, our goal to attain the status of a basic by teaching the arts as rigorous disciplines is somewhat misguided. I say "somewhat," because enriching the art curriculum has, by and large, been good in and of itself. But to be basic, the arts will have to show the corporate world that what it is asking of education is too limited for its own good. We will have to point business and the schools to a larger universe. We have to show them that the arts can serve our country and our youth in incredibly important ways—ways that will enhance education, enhance life, and, yes, enhance the ability of people to be productive citizens. We must win the schools *and* industry. If we choose not to, our status will continue to remain marginal or decline further. After all, we have as much responsibility as any other subject to make certain that the talents and human potential of children are realized, not squandered.

WAYS THE ARTS EDUCATE

The heartening news is that we already do connect with this larger educational agenda in rather startling ways, although we often prefer not to think about it. In spite of our deeply ingrained "arts for arts' sake" attitude, we actually do impart some very practical habits of thought. We do this even while we resist being useful. I want to suggest four ways in which the arts make natural and unique connections with the larger world of commerce and the deeper purposes of education. All relate directly to mentation in every art form and at the same time develop abilities that are generally not being taught through other subjects.

Thinking Aesthetically

One of the major problems of American manufacturing, perhaps its single most damaging fault, has been the loss of quality in craftsmanship and design. The Japanese and Koreans can put together a reliable, well-made product. That means that all along the line, people *care* about what they are doing. The arts teach that kind of caring. Study of any of the arts can furnish people with a crucial aesthetic metaphor of what life at its best might be. The study of music, for example, can transform the way we think and operate. It can provide an aesthetic value orientation. Ideally, the aesthetics of music become the aesthetics of life. Through the study of music, we recognize the beauty of order. We respect the striving for perfection. We appreciate how all the elements—the details—make the expressive whole and how important those details are. And in the process, we learn how to handle frustration and failure in pursuit of our goals. You want a good product? Fill the assembly line with people who think like musicians. Or artists. Or dancers.

The aesthetic awareness we learn through study of the arts becomes a way we relate to the world. Our aesthetic view becomes a natural and important part of our encounter with life. It is the way we bring our sensual and rational beings together to come to terms with the world around us. The arts are a celebration of excellence. They are the way we learn to release our positive energies toward an aesthetic result. They are the way we fuel our motivations beyond greedy self-interest. In the arts, wanting the job to be done right has nothing to do with money. (The understatement of the year!)

The important point here is the possible transfer of our aesthetic frame of reference from the arts to other realms of life, something that educators have tended to overlook. The ability to think aesthetically, applied across the board, can make a substantial difference in the quality of life. That is why the arts are *not* the domain of the privileged, the rich, or the talented, but belong to us all. It is in the best interests of business—its self-interest—to want all employees to have a substantial education in the arts. Germany and Japan do not fail their youth or their industries in this respect.

Thinking Creatively

If there is a fourth "R" that needs to be added to the traditional three, it is Reasoning (Baron & Brown, 1988). Many Americans cannot think straight, and American business is suffering for it. Here the arts can make another unique contribution. In their creative aspects particularly, the arts require a high order of abstract reasoning. Among all the subjects in the curriculum, the arts are unique in that there are very few absolutely right or wrong answers. It is precisely the ambiguities of these forms of symbolic expression that call upon us to exercise a higher order of thought processes. When is a poem, a painting, or a musical composition finished? When is the interpretation of music perfected? What makes choreography and music meld? When is a painting fully understood? What gestures best express a particular character? What is appropriate? These are the kinds of complex problems, as Elliot Eisner (1982) reminds us, that we deal with in our personal relations with others at home and in the workplace. Two-plus-two-equals-four is not akin to the kinds of difficult thinking and decision making we are required to make so often in the adult world. The arts can provide opportunities for this higher form of reasoning, if we choose to teach them so that they do.

Education in an art is an invitation to exercise the intellectual skills of an artist—to envision, to set goals, to determine technique and exercise it, to figure out, to evaluate, to revise, to continue to imagine and solve problems; in a word, to *create*. In this act, there is enormous self-discipline. American enterprise is looking for creative problem solvers, people who can think a situation through to an innovative solution (Committee for Economic Development, 1985; Task Force on Education for Economic Growth, 1983). Oddly enough, businesses have not made the connection between their need for employees who possess such problem-solving skills and the capacity of the arts to develop those skills. They fail to understand that the organic and spontaneous nature of the arts is not at odds with, but rather a complement to, their own penchant for mechanization and systematization.

That is important for us to remember, too. Problem solving in the context of the arts should be lively and engaging. It does not have to be academic in the staid definition of that term. The danger of opting to ape the academic subjects is that we will relinquish the one strong card we hold—that the arts are refreshingly different in the way they are taught and learned. In adopting an academic approach, we must be careful that we do not make the arts just as dull as many of the other subjects—just as left-brained. We actually have people advocating that students in band classes keep notebooks (College Entrance Examination Board, 1985).

We are not going to keep young people in school by giving them more drudgery. In fact, the action, delight, and personal challenge that the arts induce can be a deterrent to students' leaving school. The arts, like athletics, can make school enjoyable to students who cannot find joy anywhere else. They can touch the spirit of students whose spirit is denied in every other quarter. I do not think we should apologize because the arts are user friendly. In fact, I think that we should capitalize on it. We should let our educational and corporate leaders know that we believe we can be a factor to deter the high dropout rate that is such a concern to us all.

Thinking Communicatively

There is no effective commercial enterprise without effective communication. In an information society, if people cannot communicate, they are dead. No wonder American business is worried about our high school graduates. They have difficulty communicating because they have not been introduced to many of the *tools* of communication. All the art forms are means of expression and communication, even though the emphasis in arts education has been largely on the former. But each of the arts functions as an important and unique communication system, and education in the arts is primarily a search for meaning.

The arts are forms of thought every bit as potent in what they convey as mathematical and scientific symbols. They are the ways we human beings "talk" to ourselves and to each other. They are the languages of civilization through which we express our fears, our anxieties, our curiosities, our hungers, our discoveries, our hopes. The arts are modes of communication that give us access to the stored wisdom of the ages. Most important, they are the ways we give form to our ideas and imagination so that they can be shared with others.

When we educate our artistic intelligences, we awaken our perceptions and levels of awareness. We put more of our mind to work. We develop our capacity to view the world from different perspectives and to absorb from it more broadly. We immediately open windows to understanding. As Eisner (1982) has pointed out, when we deny children access to a major expressive mode such as music, we deprive them of "the meanings that the making of music makes possible" (p. 55). The same could be said of depriving children of access to the expressive modes of art, dance, poetry, and theatre. We deprive them of the meanings that these arts provide. We impoverish the mind. And we delimit our capacity to express and to communicate.

When we turn off these important parts of what human beings are—shut down some of the engines of life—we create an underclass of uncultured citizens. The result is a lesser human being. One of the problems of American education today is that it produces too many people who operate in very limited modes. A part of them is forever frustrated and denied. As workers, such people do not make good businesspeople, good plumbers, good salespeople, or good mayors. Can we afford another generation of lost youth?

We have many indications that the failure of schools to cultivate and refine the sensibilities has had adverse effects upon the younger generation. My observations in schools indicate that drugs, crime, hostility, indifference, and insensitivity tend to run rampant in schools that deprive students of instruction in the arts. In the process of overselling science, mathematics, and technology as the panaceas of commerce, schools have denied students something precious—access to their expressive/communicative being, the essence of their personal spirit. In inner city schools that are devoid of the arts, there is little pride and less enthusiasm. The United States will not prosper on the backs of these depleted lives.

Thinking Culturally

The other vast area that is unique to the arts is what they teach us about ourselves and other people. The arts can establish a basic relationship between the individual and the cultural heritage of the human family. As advancing systems for travel and communication bring the peoples of this world closer, understanding human differences becomes increasingly important. The foundations for peace between peoples depends on intercultural connection and exchange. Recognizing our interdependence as peoples is the backbone of commerce in today's world. How can we have real teamwork any other way?

The greatest gift one people can give to another is to share their culture. One of the most revealing ways that we do this is through the arts. Cultural artifacts breathe their origin. They tell us who *we* are and who *they* are. If we are not to be a country of many separate peoples, we must establish commonalities of culture as well as some understanding across our many distinguishable artistic legacies. If we do not find common ground, we shall perpetrate cultural separatism. To share artistic creations across cultures is to share our deepest values. Recognizing our similarities and understanding our differences gives us a base to establish cultural cohesiveness and respect, two vitally important values in a shrinking world and a world in which technology seems doggedly to deny our humanness. Science and mathematics do not provide this kind of insight.

CONCLUSION

I hope my main point is clear: I believe there are practical applications of the theory of multiple intelligences that can be useful for all students, that can place the arts solidly in the basic curriculum. I have tried to take a look at what this shared core might be like. We do not need more and better arts education to develop more and better artists, any more than we need mathematics in the core curriculum primarily to develop mathematicians. We need more and better arts education to produce better-educated human beings, citizens who will value and evolve a worthy American civilization. *Better educated human beings:* That is our justification for being an essential part of general or basic education. That is why the arts are a common heritage to be shared by all. And that is why the schools have an obligation to pass that heritage on to the next generation. Access to that heritage is a right of citizenship.

Corporate America needs to think more broadly about what makes people good employees, beyond their ability to read, write, and compute. The schools need to reach beyond mere employability. We need to show them the way. Paul E. Burke, a member of the commission on standards for school mathematics (of the National Council of Teachers of Mathematics), says, "To be educated, you need to know various habits of thought. There is a mathematical approach that works in some situations. But kids have been exposed to that for eight years before high school. And it's not the only approach. Art and history also involve certain habits of thought that are worth acquiring" (Raspberry, 1989, p. A 23). And he might have added dance, music, and theatre. Turning out citizens who recognize and respect good craftsmanship, are committed to an artistic result, and have the ability to judge their own efforts by the highest standards is an accomplishment essential to an effective work force. We need citizens who can think for themselves, communicate effectively, and understand and appreciate our ethnic diversity. The arts are a vast educational resource for teaching these competencies. They are fundamental enablers. They can play a vital role in making humans functional.

What I am suggesting is that we must take action to save our arts program from more cutbacks and our children from more deprivation. We must rescue the arts for America's children by finding ways to develop an arts-as-basic curriculum, one that will stress the ABC's of the arts for all students, one that will focus on teaching the *competencies* of the arts that serve the real *priorities* of the schools. It should be reassuring to us that the arts can serve the larger purposes of education naturally if we teach the habits of thought that are inherent within them—aesthetic, creative, communicative, cultural, and undoubtedly others. We do not have to distort the arts to serve these purposes. When it comes to basic education, the arts can hold their own.

We need to remind our business and educational leaders that artistic habits of thought contribute significantly to their interests, and we need to teach the arts so that these connections are obvious. We must learn to face our paranoia about utility and realize that we can be true to *our* purposes and useful at the same time. If we want to be basic, we have to relate to the society and the schools in which we exist. Someone said, "The last thing a sea fish discovers is salt water." Society and the schools *are* our salt water.

What America must come to understand is that we will not be a nation that is qualified until we are a nation that is cultured. The two go hand in hand. When the arts come to be viewed as intelligences that are invaluable to every human being and to the enterprises that sustain us, study of the arts will be required of all. The arts will be *made* basic. That status is not something we can ask for. It is something we must earn.

References

Baron, J., & Brown, R. (1988, August 7). Why Americans can't think straight. *The Washington Post,* p. B 3.

College Entrance Examination Board. (1985). *Academic preparation in the arts: Teaching for transition from high school to college.* New York: Author.

Committee for Economic Development, Research and Policy Committee. (1985). *Investing in our children: Business and the public schools.* New York: Author.

Eisner, E. (1982). *Cognition and curriculum: A basis for deciding what to teach.* New York: Longman.

Fowler, C. (1988). *Can we rescue the arts for America's children?* New York: American Council for the Arts.

Gardner, H. (1983). *Frames of mind: The theory of multiple intelligences.* New York: Basic Books.

Getty Center for Education in the Arts. (1985). *Beyond creating: The place for art in America's schools.* Los Angeles: Author.

National Commission on Excellence in Education. (1983). *A nation at risk: The imperative for educational reform.* Washington, DC: U.S. Government Printing Office.

National Endowment for the Arts. (1988). *Toward civilization: A report on arts education*. Washington, DC: U.S. Government Printing Office.

Raspberry, W. (1989, March 15). Math isn't for everyone. *The Washington Post*, p. A 23.

Task Force on Education for Economic Growth. (1983). *Action for excellence: A comprehensive plan to improve our nation's schools*. Denver: Education Commission of the States.

14

Summary and Coda

WILLIAM J. MOODY

In bringing this book to a close, I want to review the key points emphasized by the authors in the preceding chapters. It is my hope that this summary will enable readers to recall the import and feel the impact of the material already so cogently expressed.

THE ARTS, AESTHETICS, AND EDUCATION

The role of the arts in our culture commands the interest of all who are concerned with arts education and was an important theme of several chapters in this book. Futrell (Chapter 4) sees art as a civilizing influence that refines our capacity for understanding our neighbors who share this planet. Fowler (Chapter 13) refers to a "shrinking world" where artistic creations help people across cultures to share their deepest values.

Scientific knowledge and technological advances make it possible to air-condition our bodies, but the arts are more likely to nurture our spirit. And we hope that the spirit of oneness with the human family will give our leaders the wisdom to secure peace and preserve this planet in the face of a terrifying potential for destruction.

> Artistry, more than militancy, can give new meaning to an ideal as old as the scriptures and as compelling as the morning headlines, the ideal of peace on earth, good will toward men. And active artistic intelligences, more than strategic defense initiatives, offer the best hope that the forces of civilization will hold in check the forces of barbarism. And, in the process, save us from ourselves. And save for our children a world of beauty, a world of harmony. (Futrell, Chapter 4)

Each of the arts communicates with the soul through its own symbolic system. Even before the wonders of the written word, pictures were painted, work was sung, dreams were danced. Today we read about the wars of the past and wonder about inhumane history, while revelling in the works of art that present humankind's best efforts through the ages. What do people gaze at when they travel the world and visit its museums? How many millions attend concerts and plays? And yet it is difficult in this country for the arts to be part of "basic" education.

A nation that embraces so much violence and adulates the macho in a world where powerful individuals fuel atavistic paranoia in order to get richer, regardless of the consequences in human and environmental waste, is not fertile ground for aesthetics. But the aesthetic possibility is there for everyone, that liberating effect of wide-awakeness, "the capacity to perceive and reflect upon what is so frequently concealed by the familiar and the habitual, as well as by ignorance" (Greene, Chapter 12).

It is hard to get a grip on life, including education, when technological change is rampant; nevertheless, the future shock we face is not from scientific advances but from spiritual neglect. "In an open democracy of the kind we have been developing in the United States, we have now produced a pluralistic society in which greed, avarice, and selfishness are raised to the level of national ideals" (Taylor, Chapter 1).

Arts education has been relegated to an inferior status over the past several years and in some school systems has been dismantled. Fowler (Chapter 13) decries that the purpose of American schooling today is preparation for work, and Futrell (Chapter 4) reminds us that education should be the engine driving our economy rather than a vehicle in the hands of big business. Can the United States reach its potential if its people are not cultured? Will those who seek money or power set the direction of our curricula?

THEORY OF MULTIPLE INTELLIGENCES

In Chapter 2, Howard Gardner defines intelligence "as an ability to solve problems or to fashion a product, to make something that is valued in at least one culture." He reminds us that he started his professional career with the commonly held notion that intelligence is one all-encompassing brain activity, and explains how his research convinced him that, in fact, there are at least seven quite distinct "intelligences." He presents convincing evidence from medical research that these seven have biological origins and seem to respond to impulses specific to isolated sections of the brain. He gives experiential evidence for the seven, wondering, for example, if anyone believes that Einstein "would have been an equally creative statesman, musician, painter, or dancer."

Although it is possible for students (especially if motivated) to be bright in several areas, experienced teachers know that some students are superior in selected areas and only average (or below) in others. Vallance (Chapter 7) referred to "tacit intelligences" to describe how people process information through some intelligences and are frustrated when working in others. Will Rogers gave the commonsense view in his inimitable way—there is nothing so stupid as an educated man, if you get off the thing that he was educated in.

Gardner does not say that any intelligence is inherently artistic. The potential to be a dancer may lead instead to agility on the athletic field; sound and rhythm are concomitants of both music and poetry. In fact, all of us use intelligences in combination and are usually unself-conscious about which is used where. Kleinman (Chapter 10) writes about a "host of sensual qualities in a dizzying array and combination of impressions and feelings."

Within an art form, the dynamics of intelligence are also complex. Manual dexterity is a factor in the success of instrumental musicians, but this is not what Gardner has isolated as musical intelligence. Hoffer (Chapter 11) asks whether ability causes one to develop an interest or whether interest causes one to develop an ability.

There is no doubt that both genetic and environmental factors contribute to what we recognize as ability or competence. The importance of Gardner's theory is in the impetus it provides to organize the school environment so that (1) ability in each of the seven intelligences is targeted for general improvement and (2) strengths are identified and, consequently, special opportunities and encouragement for the gifted are provided.

IMPLICATIONS FOR EDUCATION

Even with rapid advances in technology, an expanded knowledge base supported by research, and radical changes in cultural mores, adults have an emotional attachment to schools as they remember them. Most professional educators seem to be comfortable with a school curriculum that is "fragmented into separate subjects, standardized by accreditation agencies and post-secondary institutions, unified by pedagogical methodologies, and justified by a 'sanitary' form of empirical evaluation" (Kridel, Chapter 7).

It is well past time to redefine education, to shake loose from stultified habits. Elliott (Chapter 11) divides various educational philosophies into two categories—content centered or child centered. We are in a content-centered period, regardless of the evidence in favor of providing for special abilities and interests. Gardner's theory of multiple intelligences can be a bulwark for efforts toward an expanded view of cognition that calls for an appropriate array of experiences.

There is widespread agreement with E. D. Hirsch, Jr. (1987) about the need for cultural literacy. "There is no question about learning to read, write, and compute; and I don't think there's much question that students should learn something about the history of the world and of this country, about some aspects of science, and so on" (Eisner, Chapter 3). In serving the needs of the students, however, wise teachers look for individual intelligence profiles, provide for variance in learning styles, and are concerned about special interests that may challenge students to move rapidly in one learning domain.

The political and business leaders who want to influence educational curricula seem to believe that our schools can and should produce millions of computer-literate graduates who will patriotically take their places in the front lines of scientific research. The concept of multiple intelligences confounds this view by presenting scientific evidence for a more child-centered approach leading to what Eisner (Chapter 3) calls the cultivating of "productive idiosyncrasy. . . . providing the conditions through which people become increasingly individuated and increasingly optimized with respect to their unique abilities, the particular talents they possess." The Yankee ingenuity that built this country will continue to work, and industry will have its creative geniuses, but only if schools discover and nourish children who have special abilities.

The chapters in this book do not focus on methodology, nor on the psychology of learning. Gardner's theory, however, does buttress the work of several leading educators. Vallance (Chapter 7) described discipline-based art education, an approach developed by the Getty Center for Education in the Arts (1985); she reviewed Dwayne Huebner's (1966) five rationales—technological, scientific, political, aesthetic, and ethical. Discussion among others concerned with education in the various art forms found learning styles (and modalities) walking hand in hand with multiple intelligences.

A content-centered versus child-centered curriculum is not the only dichotomy that has been noted. It has been pointed out that the arts contribute to the teaching of English, history, and science. For example, when Newman was a superintendent of schools, he observed a class and asked the students, "Are you doing science, or are you doing art?" He described their reaction as follows: "And many of them had this very puzzled look on their faces because they would be doing scientific drawing and didn't know whether they were doing science or art. And I thought that it was wonderful" (personal communication, April 22, 1989). At the same time the point has been made that the arts must be taught as separate disciplines, possibly leading to career choices. How else will children begin

> to explore our own language, to try to construct a world (as Elizabeth Bishop did) with our own pigments or sounds or gestures or words . . . to understand art-making in some fashion, to grasp "making" itself. . . . Knowing this, I believe persons are more likely to grasp the idea that they must move beyond the stance of mere spectator or consumer if they are to come into the presence of works of art. (Greene, Chapter 12)

In fact, the arts may help teach the artist. Collins found that students have difficulty expressing thoughts or visions.

> So, we've again turned to the arts to *play* with and to extend the senses through theatre games in order to help the students *see, describe, feel, react*. Pantomime is used to *show* students in a physical, participatory manner how to add information nonverbally to communicate a clear, detailed, specific idea. . . . By moving, seeing, and responding, students are learning to add detail. (Chapter 9)

There is no doubt that the educating of multiple intelligences would revolutionize schooling in the United States. We would call into question our grade structure and length of the school year. Perhaps we would see that students who are interested in a particular study have the time to do so in increments other than the standard 50 to 60 minutes. Many changes would be necessary to advance an institution that traditionally moves slowly. For instance, how do we approach the teachers? Werner (Chapter 10) reminds us that classroom teachers need in-service training to acquire skills necessary for effective use of the arts. Futrell (Chapter 4) believes that progress "may depend decisively on restructuring teacher preparation programs."

Arts education is for all children, not only for the gifted, talented, and intelligent. The arts stimulate and provoke the spirit, so it is appropriate that Gardner (Chapter 2) ended his chapter with a reminder that education must comprise more than subject matter.

> As important as intelligence is and as much as psychologists are interested in it and talk about it, character and vision and responsibility are at least as important—probably more important. How an individual goes about using his or her intelligences within a vision of society is extremely important. As Harold Taylor emphasized in Chapter 1, the arts are a very important part of this consideration. They have been from the time of Plato and Confucius to Pablo Picasso and Pablo Casals.

TESTING AND ASSESSMENT

A concern with the overemphasis of standardized test results reso- nates throughout several chapters in this book. In Chapter 5 Gardner pointed out that standardized testing answers the needs that legislators and school board members think they have rather than addressing the needs of students. In a United States that exalts competition and winning, newspaper editors compare batting averages in the educational game by publishing standardized scores. Yet across the country educators are be- ginning to alert the public to the dangers of standardized testing. Here in South Carolina, for example, Michael D. Rowls (1989) from the Univer- sity of South Carolina's College of Education explained in a letter to the editor of *The State* (South Carolina's largest newspaper) that

> These tests are inappropriate evaluation tools at the classroom level. . . . Tests such as CTBS and BSAP overlook hard-to-measure areas like citizen- ship, the attitudes children have about reading and school, moral and ethical values, and a thousand other "basics" we know are impor- tant. . . . Ask any South Carolina teacher if tests have too much influ- ence on what goes on in classrooms and the curricula of the schools. You will hear an overwhelming yes! We have lost sight of some of the truly important roles teachers and schools must fulfill for our children. (p. A–8)

In addition to such letters to the editor, which are increasingly appearing across the country, numbers of responsible editors and other media com- mentators are becoming allies against the mania and misrepresentation they helped to create.

It is testing, especially standardized testing, and not assessment that is the problem. People want to know how their children are doing so we standardize curricula and testing in order to have what Eisner (Chapter 3) terms "commensurability." Assessment, however, need not be standard- ized and can be done in a way that recognizes multiple intelligences through the introduction of a portfolio (more appropriately called a pro- cessfolio) into the classroom. When students, teachers, and parents ex- amine portfolios, they are looking at the data rather than at symbolic rep- resentations of only a small part of what is known and accomplished. Assessment becomes developmental, placing the teacher in a supportive and coaching role rather than in "the teacher-examiner–student-examinee model that has traditionally characterized teaching" (Mueller, Chapter 9). The result of this kind of assessment "can be used to motivate, document, edit, refine, develop, and extend the experience" (Kantner, Chapter 8).

There is another side to the picture, however. Consider the caveat (whether the proposition is true or not) that admission should be charged to a concert, production, or exhibit, or the public will not think the event worth attending. Perhaps the arts need standardized tests so the public will think them worthy of study. There is no doubt that accountability is part of the agenda for education. If we are not happy about the position of arts education in our schools and can get leverage through standardized tests, it may be to the advantage of arts educators to take the lead in proposing tests that will accomplish acceptable goals. Colbert (Chapter 8) points out that visual arts educators better come up with their own measurable standards or "standards will be imposed upon them by those who know far less about the visual arts."

Standardized assessment in the arts would most easily test cultural literacy, that is, facts about the artists and their works. Appreciation and artistry, the sine qua non for arts education, are much more difficult to test. Newman thinks that an effort to test in the arts would have a side benefit—forcing the art of testing to improve (Newman, personal communication, April 22, 1989). The National Endowment for the Arts advocates standardized testing in the arts in order to improve the quality and acceptance of arts education. It is up to arts educators to make these tests as good as they can be.

IMPLEMENTATION

Howard Gardner's theory of multiple intelligences adds one more persuasive argument for education in the arts. The challenge for those interested in arts education is to use Gardner's theory as a new and convincing approach among several to alter the status quo. The contributors to this book hope that educational and artistic leaders in all 50 states will work together to convince the public and the political "movers" that intelligence is something different from a muscle that grows with exercise, that educational curricula and methodology should be as advanced as scientific technology, and that, as Fowler (Chapter 13) wrote, "We will not be a nation that is qualified until we are a nation that is cultured."

In 1948, I was on a high school team that debated "Federal Aid to Education." Opponents were very concerned that, as a result of federal aid, there might be federal directives mandating curricula. At that time, local taxes paid approximately 70 percent of the school bills; the state, 25 percent; and the federal government, 5 percent. It never crossed my mind nor did it come up in the debates that 40 years later, big money, not government directives, would control education. The controllers affect curricula by offering greenback carrots (jobs and grants from business and government), and we know who the donkeys are.

Forty years ago universities provided opportunities for students to advance in knowledge and wisdom. At that time, business and industry expected to give on-the-job training to employees; the apprenticeship system was time-honored. Today schools and colleges offer this training. The change is not chiefly at the request of corporate leaders, although they benefit; in fact, educators who should know better have bought into the system (especially at the research universities). "The assumption within much of the education community is that any discipline, any instructional strategy, any reform initiative, any bold theory, can best be defended by establishing its economic utility" (Futrell, Chapter 4). But as, Futrell reminds us, curricula should be based on their educational merit, which is not subject to the vicissitudes of economic impact.

This is not to dispute that there are strong arguments for selling the arts, which are, in their packaging, big business. Industries do want to build where there are abundant cultural opportunities, and the arts are inextricably woven into one of the world's biggest businesses—tourism.

There are many ways to move the cause of arts education forward. For example, South Carolina is one of three states to have established a Joint Legislative Committee on Cultural Affairs. Keyserling (Chapter 6) describes the formation of this committee, which is a strong force providing legislative support for the arts—encouraging, expanding, and financing cultural activities in both the public and private sectors. For instance, collaborative efforts with educators led to a defined minimum program in the arts that requires teaching by arts specialists.

Good public relations and energetic political action are needed at every level—local, state, and national. In South Carolina, the Arts Commission has been in the forefront, providing effective leadership in several spheres as well as serving the arts and artists. In addition to "Artists in the Schools," the commission has collaborated in efforts to secure funding for Arts in the Basic Curriculum (ABC plan) and in efforts to build a strong Governor's School for the Arts. Williams (Chapter 6) describes other programs, such as the State Superintendent of Education's Celebration of the Arts, a program that recognizes the achievements of young artists.

The federal government through the National Endowment for the Arts and state governments through funds for education, arts commissions, state orchestras, and similar agencies are edging cautiously into major subvention of the arts. This is because music, theatre, dance, and museums cannot balance the budget through ticket sales, even with substantial help from corporations and individuals.

There is a difference between the Europeans and ourselves in our conception of the place of the arts in society. Although we have both fought and won the political battle for democracy, the Europeans have consid-

ered the arts to be part of their system of public and social services to
be subsidized by the government and made part of the vote-getting
apparatus at election time. (Taylor, Chapter 1)

Subvention of the arts is one of the most beneficial ways, qualitatively, for
government to serve the people.

Perhaps Gardner's theory will be the catalyst that, together with several new insights into methodology, will provide a convincing rationale
for major changes in our educational system. We have had our period of
reaction, and it is time to resume the revolution begun in the 1920s and
1930s as an educational outgrowth of John Dewey's (1916) philosophy.
Dewey's views might not appeal to Allan Bloom (1987), but they did
cause a "ferment of ideas" (Taylor, Chapter 1). Gardner's theory can do
the same by opening America's mind, all seven of them.

Good ideas need to be tried out before being adopted district-wide
or on a national scale. Valid concepts are often diminished or lost in reaction to educational experiments that failed. Robert Slavin's (1989) monumental critique of educational fads is but one example of this recognition
of the need for a different model of curricular change. He recommends
that school districts evaluate new methodology with experimental and
control classes before implementing sweeping curricular changes. Kridel
(Chapter 7) refers to learning laboratories (recommended by Mary Hatwood Futrell) and to charter schools (recommended by Albert Shanker)
as prudent environments in which to try out new methods.

There are models for infusion of the arts into the curriculum. Myers
(Chapter 6) describes the Ashley River Creative Arts Elementary School
as one where there is an arts-oriented approach in the basic curriculum
and where the arts are also taught separately by artists at all grade levels.
Gardner (Chapter 2) describes Project Spectrum in which a learning environment is created that involves children in a natural interaction with
materials that foster development of all the intelligences.

Slightly more than half of our states require at least one unit in the
fine arts for graduation from high school. All 50 states can have such a
requirement if leaders in the arts enlist political allies who will cooperate
in efforts to improve arts education.

An improved educational system must be financed largely through
tax dollars, but people are reluctant to vote for higher taxes. Perhaps in
the future there will be fewer multi-billion dollar weapons, freeing tax
dollars for defense of our cultural life. There is a Chinese proverb, attributed to Tehyi Hsieh, that says, The schools of the country are its future in
miniature.

References

Bloom, A (1987). *The closing of the American mind.* New York: Simon & Schuster.

Dewey, J. (1916). *Democracy and education.* New York: Macmillan.

Getty Center for Education in the Arts. (1985). *Beyond creating: The place for art in America's schools.* Los Angeles: Author.

Hirsch, Jr., E. D. (1987). *Cultural literacy: What every American needs to know.* Boston: Houghton Mifflin.

Huebner, D. (1966). Curricular language and classroom meanings. In J. B. Macdonald & R. R. Leeper (Eds.), *Language and meaning* (pp. 8–26). Washington, DC: Association for Supervision and Curriculum Development.

Rowls, M. D. (1989, April 24). School testing is overemphasized [Letter to the editor]. *The State* (Columbia, SC), p. A–8.

Slavin, R. (1989). PET and the pendulum: Faddism in education and how to stop it. *Phi Delta Kappan, 70* (10), 752–758.

ABOUT THE EDITOR
AND THE CONTRIBUTORS

INDEX

About the Editor
and the Contributors

WILLIAM J. MOODY is professor of conducting and music education at the University of South Carolina, where he was director of the School of Music from 1973 to 1990. His prior teaching experience includes 13 years at the university level and 7 years in public schools. He has been producer/conductor of the Columbia Lyric Opera since 1973. A former president of the National Band Association, he has been guest conductor, clinician, and adjudicator in 26 states. He has authored one book and 16 articles on instrumental music education. He initiated and coordinated the Artistic Intelligences Conference.

CYNTHIA COLBERT is an associate professor of art at the University of South Carolina in Columbia. Her research on children's artistic development, focusing particularly on drawing, verbal, and modeling skills, has been widely published. She has served as editor of *Arts and Learning Research,* a publication of the American Educational Research Association, and co-authored *Discover Art: Kindergarten* (1990).

CAROL COLLINS is the project coordinator of the South Carolina Arts in Basic Curriculum Plan at Winthrop College and was previously Director of Creative Arts in Education at the Eugene O'Neill Theater Center in Waterford, Connecticut. Her background includes work in a unique combination of drama, speech, writing, puppetry, and children's literature. She is not only an author and an educator, but an actor, a musician, and a puppeteer as well.

ELLIOT W. EISNER is a professor of education and art at Stanford University. He works in three fields: art education, curriculum, and educational evaluation. His books include *Educating Artistic Vision, The Educational Imagination, Cognition and Curriculum, The Art of Educational Evaluation* and *The Enlightened Eye.* He has received many awards for his work, in-

183

cluding the Palmer O. Johnson Memorial Award for the highest quality research published in Volume 2 of the *American Educational Research Journal,* a John Simon Guggenheim Fellowship, and the Manuel Barkan Memorial Award from the National Art Education Association. Twice he was invited to give the John Dewey Lecture. He is a past president of the National Art Education Association, was vice-president of the Curriculum Division of the American Educational Research Association, and is president of the International Society for Education Through Art.

CHARLES ELLIOTT is a professor of music at the University of South Carolina. He is founding editor of *Update: The Applications of Research in Music Education,* National Chairperson of the Society for Research in Music Education, and Chairman of the Executive Committee of the Music Education Research Council.

CHARLES FOWLER, a Washington, D.C.-based writer and consultant, is director of National Cultural Resources, Inc. Dr. Fowler's writings on the arts and education include books, educational materials, reports, and more than 200 articles. His latest book is *Can We Rescue the Arts for America's Children?* (1988).

MARY HATWOOD FUTRELL, a classroom teacher in Alexandria, Virginia, was president of the National Education Association from 1983 to 1989. *Ms.* magazine named Futrell one of 12 Women of the Year in 1985. *Ebony* honored her as the outstanding black business and professional person for 1984 and cited her as one of the 100 most influential blacks in America for 1985, 1986, and 1987. *The Ladies Home Journal* in 1984 named her one of the country's 100 top women. She is a tireless educational leader not only in this country but throughout the world.

HOWARD GARDNER is a research psychologist in Boston. He investigates human cognitive capacities, particularly those central to the arts, in normal children, gifted children, and brain-damaged adults. He is the author of over 250 articles in professional journals and wide-circulation periodicals. Among his nine books are *Art, Mind and Brain* (1982), *Frames of Mind* (1983), and *The Mind's New Science* (1985). At present, Gardner serves as professor of education and co-director of Project Zero at the Harvard Graduate School of Education, research psychologist at the Boston Veterans Administration Medical Center, and adjunct professor of neurology at the Boston University School of Medicine. In 1981, he was awarded a MacArthur Prize Fellowship.

MAXINE GREENE is professor of philosophy and education at Teachers College, Columbia University. She has been an active participant in and "philosopher-in-residence" at the Lincoln Center Institute for the Arts in Education for more than 15 years. She is a member of the National Academy of Education, a past president of the Philosophy of Education Society, the American Educational Studies Association, and the American Educational Research Association. Her books include *The Public School and the Private Vision* (1965), *Existential Encounters for Teachers* (1967), *Teacher as Stranger: Educational Philosophy in the Modern Age* (1973), *Landscapes of Learning* (1978), and *The Dialectic of Freedom* (1988). She has published more than 70 articles in a variety of journals and an equal number of monographs, prefaces, and chapters.

CHARLES R. HOFFER taught in the public schools of Michigan and then at the Campus School of the College for Education of the State University of New York at Buffalo. After serving as director of music for seven years for the Clayton school district in St. Louis County, Missouri, he joined the faculty of the School of Music at Indiana University, where he remained until 1984, when he moved to the University of Florida. He is the author of many books on music and music education, including *Teaching Music in the Secondary Schools* and *Understanding Music*. He is currently president of the Music Educators National Conference.

LARRY KANTNER holds a dual professorship in Art and Curriculum and Instruction at the University of Missouri–Columbia, where he has served as chair of the Art Department and is currently Director of Graduate Studies for the Department of Curriculum and Instruction. He has been the coordinator of the Art Education Program for the past 16 years. His research on children's aesthetic development has been published in journals of both art education and general education. He is the former editor of the *Journal of Multi-Cultural and Cross-Cultural Research in Art Education*, and editor of the newsletter of the International Society for Education Through Art (INSEA). He serves on the board of the National Art Education Association and as the director of the Higher Education Division, and is a member of the executive board of INSEA. In addition to his commitment to the intellectual activities of his profession, he continues to exhibit his own art.

HARRIET KEYSERLING is chairperson of South Carolina's Joint Legislative Committee on Cultural Affairs. In the state legislature, she also serves on the Ways and Means Committee, the Rules Committee, the Joint Legislative Committee on Energy, and the Nuclear Waste Consultation Committee. She chairs South Carolina Women in Government. Representative Keyserling was recipient of the South Carolina Arts Commission Elizabeth O'Neill Verner Award to the person in state government who has done the most for the arts in South Carolina.

SEYMOUR KLEINMAN is professor and coordinator of the Movement Arts Program in the School of Health, Physical Education and Recreation at Ohio State University, where he also serves as co-director of the Institute for the Advancement of the Arts in Education. He is a contributor and editor of the recently published *Mind and Body: East Meets West* and is well known for his work with the National Dance Association.

CRAIG KRIDEL is curator of the Museum of Education at the University of South Carolina and former editor of the journal *Teaching Education*. An associate professor of education, he currently participates in various curriculum development projects integrating historical music and education.

LYN ZALUSKY MUELLER is director of the Writing Improvement Network at the University of South Carolina and a state coordinator of the South Carolina Writing Project. Her background is in dance, arts education, and writing.

ROSE MAREE MYERS is the founding principal (in 1984) of the Ashley River Creative Arts Elementary School in Charleston, South Carolina. She received the Elizabeth O'Neill Verner Award from the South Carolina Arts Commission in recognition of outstanding contributions to the arts in South Carolina. She was awarded the John F. Kennedy Center for the Performing Arts Alliance for Arts Education 1988 School Administrator Award, one of nine administrators in the nation given this award for contributions to and support of the arts in education.

WARREN BENNETT NEWMAN administers the Arts in Education Program for the National Endowment for the Arts. Dr. Newman has taught at the elementary, secondary, and university levels. He was an assistant principal and curriculum coordinator in the public schools of Burbank, California, and served two years as superintendent of schools in the South Pasadena unified school district in California. He also served as administrator of research and program evaluation in the Office of the Los Angeles County Superintendent of Schools. He has approximately 26 publications and reports and has made 175 major presentations for committees, panels, and conferences.

HAROLD TAYLOR was named president of Sarah Lawrence College at age 30, a position he held from 1945 to 1959. He has also been a professional clarinetist and was president of the American Ballet Theatre, vice-chairman of the board of the Martha Graham School of Contemporary Dance, and chairman of the board of trustees of the Agnes de Mille Dance Theatre. He has written eight books including *Art and the Intellect,* and more than 300 articles, essays, and reviews.

ELIZABETH VALLANCE is the director of education at the Saint Louis Art Museum. Dr. Vallance is a noted curriculum theorist and art educator who, with Elliot W. Eisner, edited *Conflicting Conceptions of Curriculum* (1974).

PETER WERNER is a professor in the Department of Physical Education at the University of South Carolina. He has co-authored a book with Elsie Burton on academic integration entitled *Learning Through Movement* and has authored several articles on the same topic. He is an elementary school physical education specialist in movement education.

CHARLIE G. WILLIAMS has served the public school system in South Carolina as a teacher, coach, principal, and administrator for over 35 years. Dr. Williams was re-elected by the citizens to serve a third term as State Superintendent of Education beginning January 1987. Under his leadership, a 41-point program entitled Public Education in South Carolina: The Move to Quality, 1983–1987, was developed; this plan served as the blueprint for the Education Improvement Act of 1984, which includes more than 60 programs or practices designed to improve public education.

Index

189